"This is a simple book with a simple theme: insider movements are not biblical."

—**Elijah Abraham**,
Founder and Director of Living Oasis Ministries

"Morton has exposed the real Achilles heel of insider movements. This book helps us see the problems of claiming biblical support for a movement advocated by many ill-trained Western missionaries."

—**Joshua Lingel**,
Founder of i2 Ministries

"Morton has taken a topic saturated with missiological gobbledygook and made it as clear as a pane of glass. If you need clear, biblical reasons why insider movements are a giant step in the wrong direction, read this book."

—**Bill Nikides**,
teaching elder in the Presbyterian Church in America

"Whether it is a biblical blueprint for fulfilling the great commission or merely a Trojan horse for heresy, it is high time for the insider movement to be taken seriously. In this fascinating book, Morton does exactly that by unpacking and critiquing the movement's claims to biblical authority. This gracious but unapologetic turn in a conversation about biblical truth is also a call to the church to stop looking the other way, join in the conversation, and come to an informed decision."

—**Mark Durie**,
human rights activist and Anglican pastor

Insider Movements

Insider Movements
Biblically Incredible or Incredibly Brilliant?

JEFF MORTON

WIPF & STOCK · Eugene, Oregon

INSIDER MOVEMENTS
Biblically Incredible or Incredibly Brilliant?

Copyright © 2012 Jeff Morton. All rights reserved. Except for brief quotations in critical publications or reviews, no part of this book may be reproduced in any manner without prior written permission from the publisher. Write: Permissions, Wipf and Stock Publishers, 199 W. 8th Ave., Suite 3, Eugene, OR 97401.

Wipf & Stock
An Imprint of Wipf and Stock Publishers
199 W. 8th Ave., Suite 3
Eugene, OR 97401

www.wipfandstock.com

ISBN 13: 978-1-62032-218-5

Manufactured in the U.S.A.

Scripture quotations taken from the New American Standard Bible,® Copyright © 1960, 1962, 1963, 1968, 1971, 1972, 1973, 1975, 1977, 1995 by The Lockman Foundation. Used by permission. (www.Lockman.org)

For Deb

Contents

Foreword   ix
Acknowledgments   xiii
Abbreviations   xiv

Introduction   1
1   Buddhist Believers, Hindu Followers of Jesus, and Messianic Muslims   6
2   Is God an Equal Opportunity Religious Employer?   14
3   Genesis 14, You Say To-*mah*-to, I Say To-*may*-to   20
4   Second Kings 5, Rimmon-iscing   26
5   Jonah 1, Ninevah Your Business   30
6   John 4 and Acts 8, The Sounds of Silence   37
7   Acts 15, Parallel Universe?   45
8   Acts 17, By Jupiter, I Think He's Got It!   54
9   First Corinthians 7, Christian Remains   63
10   First Corinthians 9, To the Mormon I Became as a Mormon   70
11   Conversion Doesn't Mean to Put a Suit on a Frog   85
12   Biblically Incredible or Incredibly Brilliant?"   99

Appendix 1   105
Appendix 2   108

Bibliography   125

Foreword

DURING THE SECOND HALF of the twentieth century, a paradigm shift began taking place in Western missionary organizations. The uncritical adoption of cultural anthropology as a methodological tool for doing missionary work was taking root. Former methods revolved around the final authority of an inerrant scripture as a starting point of mission work. The new method is discussed in a paper read at a meeting of concerned missionaries at the Four Brooks Conference Center in Bucks County, Pennsylvania, in July 1985 (see appendix 1).

While some Christian missiologists were downplaying or ignoring the importance of a theological approach to missions to Muslims, other experts, not all of the Christian faith, insisted on the necessity and importance of a doctrinal analysis of Islam.

In one of his books, Bernard Lewis remarked:

> The Muslim doctrine of successive revelations culminating in the final mission of Muhammad led the Muslim to reject Christianity as an earlier and imperfect form of something which he, himself, possessed in the final, perfect form, and to discount Christian thought and Christian civilization accordingly. After the initial impact of eastern Christianity on Islam in the earliest period, Christian influences, even from the high civilization of Byzantium, were reduced to a minimum. Later, by the time that the advance of Christendom and, the retreat of Islam had created a new relationship, Islam was crystallized in its ways of thought and behavior and had become impervious to external stimuli, especially those coming from the millennial adversary in the West.

Early in 2005, I received two communications from missionaries laboring in Muslim-dominated areas who asked for my advice concerning the use of Arabic terms that refer to the Lord Jesus Christ. One missionary alerted me to the fact that in his field, some mission workers associated with an Evangelical organization were attempting to spread a "Muslim-friendly version of the Arabic Bible." The time-honored Arabic translation known as the Smith-Van Dyke version was considered inadequate in a Muslim field. The protagonist for the Muslim-friendly translation wanted to alter certain fundamental terms describing our Lord by substituting for them Arabic words that did not convey the exclusive divinity of Jesus Christ. Immediately I sent him a copy of "A Statement of Missionary Concern."

The following are excerpts from his response:

> Dear Rev. Madany,
>
> The "Statement of Missionary Concern" has certainly helped me to tease apart the humanistic trends that are entering the enterprise of missions, and has certainly called me back to a closer walk with the Lord and His word. Thank you.
>
> I am completely rethinking the approach, as I realize that much of the felt-needs approach is very human centered and does not presuppose the absolute hostility of fallen man to the truths of the Gospel. I have grown increasingly appalled—spurred on also by your insights—of the uncritical and un-Biblical stance that many well-meaning Christians have taken. May God give us courage to be 21st century Reformers. Once again, thank you for all of your input to date. It has been most valuable.

Reading various papers and publications of some Neo-Evangelicals who are clamoring for a Copernican revolution in missions to Muslims, the conclusion can be drawn that they seek not the reformation of missionary methods such as those Roland Allen sought to establish early in the past century, when he pointed out that the paternalism of several missionary agencies was in conflict with St Paul's missionary methods; rather, they are advocating a totally new missiology that parts company with the fundamentals of Christian missions across the centuries. It brings to mind the comments of the late F. F. Bruce who referred to this growing anti-traditional spirit in his book, *Tradition Old and New*.

> "Hold fast to the traditions," wrote Paul to the Christians in Corinth. Yet some would regard freedom from any kind of tradition as the sign of spiritual maturity and emancipation. That is because of the mistaken idea that tradition is always bad.

Yet the living tradition, the continuity of Christian life, is indispensable. Without it, Scripture would have had no context. If we could suppose that the church had been wiped out in the Diocletian persecution and the church's scripture lost, to be rediscovered in our own day like the Dead Sea Scrolls, would the rediscovered scriptures once more have the effect which we know them to have in experience, or would they, like the Scrolls, be an archeological curiosity and a subject of historical debate?

On the other hand, the living tradition without the constant corrective of Scripture, (or, in more modern language, without the possibility of "reformation according to the Word of God"), might have developed out of all recognition if it did not have indeed slowly faded and died.

As you read *Insider Movements: Biblically Incredible or Incredibly Brilliant?*, I trust you will capture Bruce's admonition: tradition that is not informed by scripture and scripture removed from its tradition and context, produce something other than Christianity.

Rev. Bassam Michael Madany
November 15, 2011

Acknowledgments

There were many who encouraged me in many ways. Thanks to Bill Nikides and Joshua Lingel for their ideas and friendship.

Thanks also to Adam Simnowitz, Elijah Abraham, Phil DeHart, and Fred Farrokh for reading through the manuscript at various times, all with various degrees of reticence.

Those who helped me think through some important points along the way, helping me to think more clearly were Tom McCormick, Bassam Madany, David Talley, David Garner, and Paul Lehmann.

Ultimately, I must bear the blame for anything that is in error, poorly written or miscommunicated—though I'm willing to share the praise with those who have helped. I do not say this out of a sense of humble pride or political correctness, but a with real sense of gratitude for those who have contributed to the shaping of my thoughts and this book—and so they don't sue me later, of course.

Abbreviations

IJFM, *International Journal of Frontier Missions*
MF, *Mission Frontiers*
NICNT, New International Commentary of the New Testament
SFM, *St Francis Magazine*
TNAC, The NIV Application Commentary
TNTC, Tyndale New Testament Commentary

Introduction

I WAS PRIVILEGED TO be part of the editorial committee for the i2 Ministries publication, *Chrislam: How Missionaries Are Promoting an Islamized Gospel* (2011). A compilation of eighteen authors critiquing the insider movements (IM) from various facets, the book is not an easy read if you are unfamiliar with certain Islamic, theological and missiological terms. I believe you'll find this book easier to read. That is not to say I have simply taken the guts of *Chrislam* and jiggled them a bit, cut off the fat and bone to create a slimmer, no sugar added, more efficient version of *Chrislam*. This book is different on many counts from its predecessor.

First, the passionate tone of *Chrislam* is not here. I am writing in a much more sanguine voice since my audience is different. Assuming you know nothing about insider movements and you have not dared to pick up the weighty *Chrislam*, I believe the person who reads this is much more the typical Christian who struggles with his prayer life (as I do), has trouble with his kids, or struggles just to stay ahead of Uncle Sam and keep food on the table. I wanted to write so you wouldn't have to park a dictionary nearby as if this were some manuscript from the darkness of the seventh century.

Second, this is indeed light reading. Whereas *Chrislam* is heavy with footnotes, references to many other works, charts with foreign languages, and some fairly complicated vocabulary at times, I have deliberately minimized the number of footnotes.[1] There are a few tables and figures in the book, but I've kept them to a minimum, tried to fully explain them, and as an added bonus, all the tables and figures are in English! You don't

---

1. But like it not, there are some things I just have to get off my chest that don't belong in the main body of the book—like this.

need to read Arabic or know much about Islam in order to get the most out this book.

That is not to say this is pop theology for the masses. It is my hope that while readable, the book makes you think, provides solid biblical, theological thinking, and asks the right questions in a way that is friendly and winsome. I only wish there were some type of "satire-font" that automatically displayed the occasionally appearing satire and irony. I trust you'll be able to pick up on it without the tip-off from a font.

My aim for this book is to make you feel like the two of us are sitting with a cup of coffee at a too-loud café as the bluish haze of pipe smoke layers the room (I don't smoke, but I enjoy the smell of pipes). We are two friends earnestly engaged with each other. The conversation is full of solid theology, personal information, sarcasm and wit, so that when you put down your final cup and walk away from the café, you've enjoyed every word, every sip, and every gesture. I know I will have.

And third, this book has fewer topics of discussion. *Chrislam* approached the insider movements from five perspectives: theology, missiology, translation, hermeneutics, and personal experience. You will find the major theme of this very short introduction to insider movements is simply to ask, "What does the Bible say about it?"

As the three editors of *Chrislam* worked together, we realized very early in the process that the book would have a fairly limited appeal due to its critical nature. Therefore, the idea for a simpler, more user friendly book about insider movements was discussed. This is close to what we had in mind.

It is my hope this short introduction to the insider movements will help you begin to grasp the length and breadth of the problem. I hope to persuade you that support for the activities that pass as mission strategies among the proponents of insider movements must stop; and that the theologizing among the proponents of IM is generally in question. My ultimate hope is to be honest, fair, measured in my assessment, and to honor the Lord Jesus Christ by doing so.

HOW IMPORTANT IS THIS DEBATE IN MISSIONS?

You may not know very much about the insider movements. Needless to say, it has nothing to do with Wall Street or digestion. But maybe you've heard the rumblings taking place in the Presbyterian Church of

America over translation matters.[2] You may have read an article or two in Christianity Today[3] or World Magazine[4]—then again maybe you haven't. Either way, the discussion among converts from Islam, missionaries, professors of missions, scholars of Islam, and mission organizations, is real, gathering steam, and has yet to see resolution.

One of the most prolific of the advocates of IM is Kevin Higgins, the executive director of Global Teams, a mission organization in California that plants churches among Muslims. About the IM he says, "I see Insider Movements as fueling (and being fueled by) a rediscovery of the Incarnation, of a thoroughly biblical approach to culture and religion, of the role of the Holy Spirit in leading God's people to 'work out' the gospel in new ways, and of an understanding of how God works in the world *within and beyond His covenant people*"[5] (emphasis mine).

If Kevin is right, there is a lot at stake. Timothy Tennent even wonders if the "Insider movements may be an example of a sovereign initiative that has caught us by surprise."[6] If the IM is a reformation along the lines of *the* Reformation, the last thing I want to do is stand in the way of godly men and women on God's mission. If God is at work in a marvelous way, I don't want to be the speed bump that slows things down. No one, least of all me, has the ambition to become the Johann Eck or Leo X to the Luthers of the IM.

So we have to get this right. There must be clear, biblical thinking that honestly deals with the issues. Furthermore, I want to treat fairly those with whom I disagree.

IM: A MOVING TARGET?

One of the issues not addressed in *Chrislam*, and which I will only briefly mention here, is the fluidity of IM's ideology. IM is not a monolith of principles and practices, but comprises various viewpoints on virtually everything to do with missions to Muslims. In fact, my understanding of insider movements is that it is not really a movement at all, but a set of

---

2. PCA, Overture 9.
3. Hanson, "The Son and the Crescent."
4. Belz, "Inside Out."
5. Higgins, "The Key," 155–56.
6. Tennent, "Followers," 102.

observations that are supported by biblical passages interpreted through the grid of the social sciences.

Basic to any movement is its self-identification. The advocates of IM are still hammering that out, although there are two definitions that dominate others. Kevin Higgins gives the first: "A growing number of families, individuals, clans, and/or friendship-webs becoming faithful disciples of Jesus within the culture of their people group, including their religious culture. This faithful discipleship will express itself in culturally appropriate communities of believers who will also continue to live within as much of their culture, including the religious life of the culture, as is biblically faithful. The Holy Spirit, through the Word and through His people will also begin to transform His people and their culture, religious life, and worldview."[7]

Rebecca Lewis, the wife of Tim Lewis who is the international director of Frontiers, is a scholar in her own right. She defines IM this way:

> Insider movements can be defined as movements to obedient faith in Christ that remain integrated with or *inside* their natural community. In any insider movement there are two distinct elements:
>
> 1. The gospel takes root within *pre-existing communities* or social networks, which *become* the main express of 'church' in that context. Believers are not gathered from diverse social networks to create a 'church.' New parallel structures are not invented or introduced.
>
> 2. Believers retain their identity as members of their socio-religious community while living under the Lordship of Jesus Christ and the authority of the Bible.[8]

There are certainly common elements to each definition: we are looking at a movement (rapidly moving group conversion as opposed to individual); contextualization of the gospel; faithfulness to Jesus; and the importance of one's previous cultural and religious identity. The other commonality between the two is that they are anchored to anthropological assumptions. The major differences between the definitions seem to be that Higgins emphasizes faithful discipleship within the believing community, while Lewis focuses on the element of the movement-*ness*

---

7. Higgins, "The Key," 155.
8. Lewis, "Insider Movements," 16.

and church as organically related to already existing social structures. Okay, I promise: that's as technical as I get.

Another fluid aspect of IM is that the advocates are beginning to move away from the term itself. The term *insider movements* appears to be fading and in its place are *Jesus movements, the Kingdom paradigm, movements to Jesus, incarnational movements*, and even *best practices*. It looks to me like the advocates of IM are fumbling around in the definition box in order to be accurate with their definition; however, some of my fellow critics of IM may see ulterior motives—escaping the wrath of supporters, changing the language so as to allow some breathing room or distance from controversy, and so forth—but I don't believe this to be the case. Frankly, whatever the terms used to define and describe the insider movements, if the Bible doesn't support it, I will continue to speak out against it. Fluid or solid, liquid or gas, whatever it might be, the insider movements is here. Welcome to the discussion.

1

Buddhist Believers, Hindu Followers of Jesus, and Messianic Muslims

BEHIND IM REASONING

Buddhist believers, Hindu followers of Jesus, and Messianic Muslims: this is what Western missionaries are telling us is happening in the 10/40 window. The missionaries are encouraging us to rejoice with them since God is doing something wonderful. These are movements to Jesus they tell us. These are believers who have entered the kingdom of God, yet have not changed their religion they insist. H. L. Richard explains: "If you are in a Muslim community, or a Buddhist Community, or a Hindu community, you maintain that identity in that socio-religious community. That is where you work out your discipleship to Jesus. You follow Jesus as a Hindu, as a Muslim, as a Buddhist, or whatever other variety of socio-religious community you might be from."[1]

And why should they change their religions? After all, insider movements is considered a *best practice* by many missionaries, which means it is now normative that Buddhists, Hindus, and Muslims remain in their respective socio-religious structures in order to facilitate a contextualized witness of the gospel. It looks like it has become the default setting for the missionary mandate machine.

It's obvious to anyone who can fog up a mirror that the major issues of IM appear to be socio-religious identity, socio-religious communities

1. Richard, "Unpacking," 176.

and certain forms of religious expression. I believe these are primarily anthropological concerns. They are not matters of the gospel itself—important as they might be—but issues missionaries bring to the scriptures. I will work through these matters in the coming chapters, but they are not really the focus of this book.

I believe it's important to get at the assumptions hiding behind the reasoning for IM. These assumptions will lead us to the scriptures, which I believe is the key issue for rightly understanding IM. There are many of these assumptions that drive the advocates toward their conclusions, but I think the three I discuss here will, for the most part, help shed light on the thinking, theological processes, and strategies that have been identified with IM:

- *Theology of religions*: How does the Bible inform our view of Islam? How one understands non-Christian religions affects our behavior, methodology and hermeneutic of scripture, that is, the way we interpret the Bible.

- *Scriptures*: Proponents of IM tell us scripture supports insider movements. That's fine; we would expect nothing less. But which passages and why? This is where we find their assumptions bubbling to the surface; assumptions about the role and purpose of the scriptures. Is the Bible a proof text? Does it provide parallels for missions today?

- *Conversion*: What does conversion look like? And what is it? Is there a biblical form of conversion?

I think discussing the assumptions or hidden and often undefined issues will be helpful as we work through the ramifications of the insider movements. If I can adequately flesh out the unspoken assumptions that lie behind some of the IM thinking, this will act as a background to more easily understand the themes and issues that inhabit the movement.

IM'S ASSUMPTIONS

Theology of Religions

Theology of religions (TR) is concerned with having a biblical view of religion. The bulk of this book speaks to developing a theology of religions in light of the claims of IM. There are many questions at work here. The most common has to do with soteriology (or salvation; that's the last time you'll see that technical word in this book). What does it mean to say Jesus is the only way to the Father? Do non-Christians have to actually hear the name of Jesus? Is there enough truth and revelation in other religions to bring people to Jesus? These questions are generally answered with a three-pronged model: exclusivism, inclusivism, and pluralism. It's not my purpose to discuss these here.[2]

Remember, we are dealing with assumptions, and the assumption that seems to haunt much of the writings of the advocates of the insider movements is not about the saving ability of Jesus; rather there seems to be a fascination with and appreciation for Islam that feels awkward to the general reader. It's an enthrallment that does not fit with the idea of missions to Muslims. Reading about Islam from some of the proponents of IM is like opening a jar of mayonnaise that is just beginning to spoil. It looks fine. It doesn't smell bad, but when you taste it there's something not quite right. Let me illustrate what I mean. Mazhar Mallouhi, a convert from Islam, writes about those who are Muslim followers of Jesus: "They do not see that faith in Jesus as Lord requires them to automatically renounce all they previously learnt about God, or to denounce their culture, community and family as evil."[3]

There, you've just opened that jar of mayonnaise. It looks edible, but is it? It seems like a very nice way to approach Islam. But when I read this I start to wonder what a Muslim learns about God in his religion. Does he learn that God so loved the world that he sent his Son? Does a Muslim experience the God who is love? Does he discover that God walked in the garden with Adam and Eve, appeared to Moses, Abraham, Judah, and others? Does the God of Islam, *Allah*, even desire that his children call him father? Mallouhi's idea that converts are not required "to automatically renounce all they previously learnt about God" implies the revelations of the Qur'an are trustworthy—at least to a point—and that they are part of the fabric of his new understanding of *Yahweh* (I'll use God's personal name a lot to distinguish him from the Allah of the Qur'an). The

---

2. The number of books on theology of religions is vast, so I am simply listing one representative for each of the three prongs. There are certain nuances to the exclusivist and inclusivist views, but they are not necessary for this discussion. For a representative of exclusivism see Lesslie Newbigin (*The Gospel in a Pluralistic Society*, 1989); inclusivism, see Karl Rahner (*Theological Investigations*); and for pluralism, see John Hick (*God and the Universe of Faiths*, 1973).

3. Mallouhi, " Comments," 4.

Buddhist Believers, Hindu Followers of Jesus, and Messianic Muslims　9

assumption then, is that for many proponents of IM, Allah and Yahweh is the same God. Having a robust and biblical theology of religions really helps out at this point.

Islam is a religion that is anti-Christianity. Islam teaches we do not need a mediator or a savior since the 'Isa of the Qur'an is merely a human prophet and we are born without sin (in fact, all humans are born as Muslims); simply keeping the five pillars is *good enough* for gaining paradise; Allah has no son, is not a trinity, and is not immanent as the Bible describes Yahweh. Actually if you pressed me into a corner and threatened me with brussel sprouts, I would have to say the only characteristic Allah and Yahweh share is that of Creator. Beyond this lone commonality, I know of no other similarities.[4] Therefore, my own conclusion is that Islam is a *false religion* with a *false message* about a *false hope* delivered by a *false prophet*, and written in a book filled with *false claims*.[5]

And what about Allah? Paul describes him in 1 Corinthians 8:4b-6: "We know that there is no such thing as an idol in the world, and that there is no God but one. For even if there are so-called gods whether in heaven or on earth, as indeed there are many gods and many lords, yet for us there is *but* one God, the Father, from whom are all things and we *exist* for Him; and one Lord, Jesus Christ, by whom are all things, and we *exist* through Him" (NASB).[6]

This is, I believe, a biblical theology of religions with regard to Islam. Islam is a false religion, Allah is not Yahweh, and 'Isa is not our Lord through whom all things exist. Right now this may sound like a loaded, emotional reaction to Islam, but there is more to this in coming chapters.

Scripture

The next assumption inherent to the advocacy of IM is how one views the scriptures; especially how one handles the scriptures that seem to bolster

4. You may be thinking that both Allah and Yahweh are one and the same, but the Islamic doctrine of *tauhid*, the deity's oneness, makes Allah a monad, whereas Yahweh is Father, Son, and Holy Spirit. So even when the Muslim declares the oneness of God and the Christian recites the *shema* of Deuteronomy 6:4, the oneness we both proclaim is completely dissimilar.

5. For a dated, but academic appraisal of Islam: H. A. R. Gibb's *Mohammedanism* (Oxford, 1949). Kenneth Cragg's *Islam from Within* (Wadsworth, 1980) is irenic compared to Gibb's academic tone. For an edgier approach to Islam, see Malise Ruthven's *A Very Short Introduction to Islam* (Oxford, 2000).

6. All Scripture citations unless otherwise mentioned are from the NASB.

one's view and therefore provide the necessary biblical foundation. I will discuss the scriptures as a separate assumption here, but the rest of the book is an exploration of the assumption as it merges with a theology of religions. In other words, as I work through some of the TR issues, the scriptures will be our workshop. I'm confident you'll begin to see the problems connected to the IM interpretation of the scriptures once we begin to really examine them.

Rebecca Lewis makes her assumption about the scriptures very clear:

> I hope we can make the same decision that the apostles did in Acts 15. They welcomed Greek pagans as followers of Christ without requiring the Greek believers to adopt their own religious expression of that faith, opening the way of faith for all non-Jewish people groups. Let us boldly affirm that apostolic decision and say: "God who knows the heart shows that he accepts Muslim and Hindu believers by giving the Holy Spirit to them, just as he did to us. He made no distinction between us and them for He purified their heart by faith . . . We believe that it is by the grace of our Lord Jesus that we are saved, just as they are . . . therefore, we should not make it difficult for people in other religious cultures who are turning to Christ.[7]

Lewis' point is that what God has done in Acts among Greek polytheistic pagans, he is doing today among monotheistic Muslims. Using Acts 15 as a foundation, she understands the church's decision, which prevented the gentile expression of Christianity from becoming Jewish, to apply to the church today. In other words, we must not insist that Muslim followers of Jesus become Western. The integrity of the gospel means we will evangelize Muslims by speaking of Jesus, not by preaching *churchianity*. And further, Muslims remaining in their socio-religious context actually maintains the integrity of the gospel.

Of course we shouldn't preach churchianity, but this is not where the problem of the interpretation resides. Remember, I'm trying to help you see the unstated assumption behind what she says. I direct you to one thing that consistently appears through Lewis' article—an article you may never read, but should. The article presents a view of how scripture in general should be understood. For some of the proponents of IM, scripture is less the revealed articulation of how God has dealt with his people; rather it seems scripture is something to be modeled—especially

---

7. Lewis, "Integrity," 47.

the book of Acts. Now you may be shaking your head over this. You may be thinking Morton is confused, misguided or just plain wrong. Let me explain what I mean.

This interpretation of the scriptures incorporates the influence of anthropology. I must confess as a missiologist trained to incorporate anthropology into my research, I am often guilty of the same practice: the Bible, especially the book of Acts, is a collection of stories that confirms the contextualization process of the missionary endeavor. It therefore requires that the exegete bring all his anthropological tools to it for proper understanding of what God has done and will continue to do. This is not an unusual approach for a missiologist. What's wrong here?

The Bible is indeed a collection of stories (and other genres, of course) that reveal what God has done through a particular people culminating in the fulfillment of that work in the eternal Son, the Messiah, who is the Lamb of God. Does that mean there is nothing about culture, contextualization, syncretism, and the like? Of course not, but the thrust of the story of the Bible is not how do we twenty-first century Christians make the gospel relevant. Relevancy is an anthropological assumption (from Charles Kraft and communication theory). My assumption about the gospel story is that it is a *transformational message*. The Bible, especially Acts, records the unique events of the church's history as it encountered and confronted culture, and as it changed culture. Therefore, it must be interpreted in light of this context.

I believe the view of the scriptures for many of IM's proponents is to ask, "How do we make it relate to the culture at hand?" It's not that this is a bad question, but there is a better question. In light of the scripture's message of transformation and confrontation, how do I understand what is taking place in the context of the first century? Let's determine the real sense of what's taking place in the story before we try to make it apply to our context. And you know what? The story may not actually apply to our situation in the way we think.

Conversion

The final assumption concerns conversion. Conversion is an assumption? How can something we are praying for, something that is part of the whole enchilada of what we are working toward be an assumption?

Normally when we speak of conversion, we are thinking of the biblical word *epistrephō*: to turn. We think of making a u-turn away *from* our sinful past and turning *to* the Savior; however, this is not the assumption of some of the advocates of IM. What the advocates seem to believe is that when the critics of IM speak of conversion, we mean taking on Western Christianity's forms and theology, sometimes referred to as *Christianity* by the advocates of IM, as evidence of a new life. In other words, one of the major presumptions for some IMers is that those us who do not understand IM may be asking Muslims to become westernized Christians as evidence of their conversion.

Are you shaking your head? You should be. Here again is advocate of IM, Rebecca Lewis, making her case for what conversion is in a discussion of the early church's decision not to Judaize gentile believers: "Therefore, they [the apostles] did not oppose it or add on demands for religious conversion [of the gentiles]. If we use the same two criteria today, insider movements affirm that people do not even have to go through the religion of Christianity, but only through Jesus Christ, to enter God's family."[8]

The unspoken assumption is that missionaries who disagree with the IM paradigm are squeezing new converts from Islam into the Western mold of conversion that is Christianity. And perhaps more poignant, there is the assumption that insider movements don't do that. IM does not force new believers into a churchianity mold. IM is therefore more biblical, more God-honoring. The first assumption (that missionaries are squeezing Muslims into a Western mold as if it is the norm) couldn't be farther from reality. I have been a missionary for more than twenty-five years and have yet to meet a missionary that does what the advocates of IM assume. In fact, just the opposite is true. Missionaries are trained to be aware of their own cultural baggage in order to proclaim Jesus. They are educated to look for bridges and various means of contextualization in order to be able to preach the gospel. The advocates of IM who assume the worst of fellow missionaries have created a straw man case. Missionaries are forcing conversions through a Western grid, the advocates of IM believe. We all agree this is a wrong approach to conversion. And what of the second assumption? Sorry, but you will have to wait until chapter 11 for this discussion.

---

8. Lewis, "Insider," 18.

There are several other assumptions that are worthy of mention: the role of identity, the understanding of the nature and definition of the church, and the translation of the biblical familial terms of *Father* and *Son*, just to name just a few. Unfortunately, these are not the topics discussed in this book. But in the remaining chapters I want to examine these three main assumptions I've already laid out: theology of religions, the foundational scriptures of IM (with a brief look at how scriptures are used) and conversion.

2

Is God an Equal Opportunity Religious Employer?

THERE'S A NEW SHERIFF IN TOWN

WHAT IS YOUR THEOLOGY of religions (TR)? You probably haven't given it much thought, right? You believe Jesus is Lord and Savior; he died for our sins, and on that basis people go to heaven. Your theology of religions is probably wrapped up in John 14:6. Most of us don't give a theology of religions much more thought than that. It hardly seems worth the while, that is, until someone comes along and challenges the status quo. But in the world of missions to Muslims, TR is important; and there is a new theology of religions in town. It has captured the townspeople's fancy—as do most new ideas.

My purpose in the next eight chapters is first, to help you see the theology of religions that is being championed by some of the advocates of the insider movements; and second, to offer an opposing point of view. But in the end, it's up to you to decide which perspective "wears the badge."

ISLAM IS NOT EMBRACEABLE, BUT TRANSFORMABLE

Kevin Higgins has written more than most advocates of IM about Islam as a religion. He has some interesting opinions about Islam. I certainly agree with him when he states that Islam is not something a Christian can accept as valid: "It is obvious that I am a supporter of insider movements. . . .

Is God an Equal Opportunity Religious Employer? 15

I am not saying that Islam as we know and experience it—nor even in its supposedly pure or orthodox form—is 'true,' or that it can be embraced as it is by a believer."[1]

But then the waters of clarity are muddied by backtracking from the initial statement when Higgins writes this: "it is . . . possible . . . an 'original Islam' . . . has been lost through the misinterpretation of what became the 'orthodox' versions."[2] From here he goes on to ruminate that the original, orthodox version of Islam, much closer to what we think of as Christianity, may one day be restored to it's vestigial virginity—that is not how he describes, but it is my take—by Messianic Muslims, that is by Christians who remain within the embrace of Islam's culture. Imagine: Islam reformed from within. Perhaps we are indeed on the brink of a Reformation catching us unaware (my satire font failed me here).

CRASH LANDING IN NO MAN'S LAND

So, just where does Higgins land on the truth and goodness spectrum of Islam as a religion? In other words, how much of Islam is good and how much is false? He states: "If I am convinced, for example, that Islam is a demonic and deceptive lie conceived by Satan, this will certainly affect the biblical, theological, and historical material I draw from and how I apply it. On the other hand if I conclude that Islam is the final truth from God, or an equally valid expression of 'truth,' this too would affect how I look at the Bible, the early development of Christian theology, and the history of the church."[3]

Actually he never really comes right out and says if he believes either view of Islam, does he? But by posing the two extremes (see Figure 1), I'm guessing he believes Islam is neither demonic nor the last best hope for mankind, the mother of all truth. Therefore he must land somewhere in between.

Figure 1. Extremes on a Christian perspective on Islam.

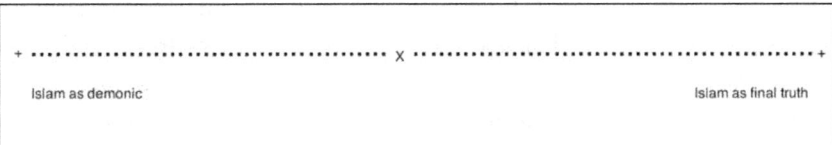

1. Higgins, "Acts 15," 38.
2. Ibid., 40.
3. Higgins, "Identity," 120.

The "X" in Figure 1 is as likely a place as any that Higgins might say is his understanding of Islam. It's a nice, safe, moderate position. It's not too Talibanish to the right and not too Fundamentalist on the left. But what does scripture say?

Since the Bible says nothing explicitly about Islam, it's best if we back up and look at the big picture of scripture. At the heart and soul of the biblical message is the incarnation of Jesus, the vehicle for God's mercy, grace, and the gospel of the kingdom. The Apostle John tells us "this is the testimony, that God gave us eternal life, and this life is in his Son. Whoever has the Son has life; whoever does not have the Son of God does not have life" (1 John 5:11–12). Eternal sonship and the incarnation are at the hub of the biblical testimony of God. Eternal life comes to those who have the Son of God, the one who came in the flesh, fully human and fully divine.

What does Islam say about the Son and his incarnation? Muhammad received this revelation from Allah: "And the Christians call Christ the Son of God. That is a saying from their mouth in this they but imitate what the unbelievers of all used to say, *God's curse be on them,* how they are deluded away from the truth" (Q9:30,[4] emphasis mine).

1 John 5:11–12 and Q9:30 stand in stark contrast to each other, as different as Allah the Merciful is from Yahweh. On the one hand the Bible tells us there is life in the Son; on the other hand, the Qur'an curses those who say Allah has a son. The most important thing to notice then is that the Bible and the Qur'an stand in direct opposition to each other on the idea of the Son and life. The Sonship of Jesus is not some small peripheral idea. The concept that *the Son has life* is not just a nice thought that really doesn't matter. Nothing could matter more! In fact if the Bible and the Qur'an differ on this—the very heart and soul of the gospel message—this chasm of difference swallows up as irrelevant any agreements on doctrine the two books may share.

We are not finished with John's take on the possibility that Islam or any religion has truth in it. First he told us there is life in the Son; second, he wrote, "every spirit that does not confess Jesus is not from God. This is the spirit of the antichrist, which you heard was coming and now is in the world already" (1 John 4:3). If this statement does not apply to Islam—that Islam is a religion in the spirit of antichrist—then why bother to have a Bible?

---

4. All qur'anic citations come from `A. Yusuf `Ali's, *The Meaning of the Holy Qur'an* and are abbreviated with Q followed by the *sura* (chapter) and *aya* (verse).

A POLITICALLY *INCORRECT* STATEMENT

So let me rework Figure 1, now cleverly renamed Table 1. In one sense Figure 1 gives us a legitimate dichotomy, but it needs some exploration. Is Islam, or any religion for that matter, in the spirit of antichrist? What is needed is a biblical measurement; therefore Table 1 measures Islam against the Word of God with the biblical standard of 1 John 5:11–12 and 4:3. Furthermore, notice I've removed any notion of a spectrum or sliding scale of possibilities. The chart is deliberately contrastive: black and white, this or that, truth or falsehood.

Table 1. The black and white of two religions.

Christianity	Islam
The teaching: God has a son and in the son is life	*The teaching*: God has no son and saying so brings a curse
The result: having the Son means having life	*The result*: delusion

When the Christian uses the Bible to weigh the message of Islam, I believe there can be no confusion. I'm sorry this next statement is not politically correct, that it's not sensitive to the vast majority of Muslims who are wonderful people and truly likeable; that it may not be the most civilized way of speaking, but the Word of God makes it quite obvious: *Islam has the spirit of antichrist*. If we use Figure 1 to ask the question, "What do we think of Islam?" we may indeed land in the middle, thinking Islam has a little bit of truth and little bit of falsehood. That question leads us into a theology of religions that is biblically incoherent. This type of thinking puts us in no man's land: a place of infertility, confusion, even syncretism. This is no way to run a theology of religions. That badge is tarnished. It's time to hire a different sheriff.

YAHWEH, DEMONS, AND REBELLION

Higgins has other things to say about religions that reveal his TR. I tend to agree with most of his general observations, but when Higgins gets to Islam, I believe he lets down his guard. Kevin has a godly desire to see Muslims come to Christ, but it looks as if he allows his emotions to take control of his understanding of scripture.

Higgins makes three basic statements about religion that are relevant to the discussion. His first two statements are sound, but these are followed by a third that troubles me. First he writes, "We find biblical evidence that religion is seen as the rejection of the truth of God."[5] Second, he believes some religious activity involves the demonic. So far, so good; I agree. Thirdly he writes—and notice the disconnect from the previous two statements—"God is at work in other religions,"[6] meaning that some adherents of other religions are in relationship to Yahweh.

Do you find this troubling? I do. On the one hand it seems the Bible is clear that religion is a rejection of God and the truth about God. There is even the presence of the demonic in religious activity, and yet despite these two solidly biblical statements, it then seems possible to conclude that God is at work in other religions?

Again, for the sake of clarity, the claim is made that Yahweh is knowingly—certainly it would never be unwittingly—at work within demonic-plagued, rebellion-filled religions. Yahweh is willing to use other religions, no matter how demonic, even if they have the spirit of antichrist, to establish relationships with certain people.

Have you ever seen a septic tank that is full? A full-to-the-brim septic tank is a terrible sight—and smell—and an unfortunate, but very accurate picture of religion. Can you imagine Joe, your friendly, local septic tank maintenance guy, swimming inside your septic tank because you told him you lost your Timex? And all the while Joe is searching for the Timex, you are wearing a diamond studded Rolex. Why should Joe jump into that filth to retrieve a thirty-dollar watch when you have an expensive, highly desirable piece of jewelry on your wrist?

Would the most holy Creator choose to walk around in filthy, disease-ridden sewage of religions in order to establish a relationship with a person when he has already given us his incomparable Son? Surely I can't be the only one to wonder how it is that Yahweh chooses to operate in such a hostile work environment. Is he an equal opportunity religious employer? Well, maybe he *doesn't* choose to work there.

How do the proponents come to this conclusion? This is the question that drives the rest of the book.

---

5. Higgins, "Inside What?" 84.
6. Ibid., 85.

3

Genesis 14, You Say To-*mah*-to, I Say To-*may*-to

THE ADVOCATES OF INSIDER movements insist they have some biblical justification for their views. What follows are the major passages that provide the foundation for their views, especially as they pertain to a theology of religions. The main questions addressed are these: Does Yahweh work in other religions? Is there even a smattering of truth in other religions that Yahweh can manipulate in order to bring people to himself?

The conclusion of some proponents of IM is that Yahweh does use other religions. He is at work inside those religions. Not everything in Islam is demonic; some things within Islam are salvageable.

GENESIS 14:17–20

17 Then after his [Abram's] return from the defeat of Chedorlaomer and the kings who were with him, the king of Sodom went out to meet him at the valley of Shaveh (that is, the King's Valley). 18 And Melchizedek king of Salem brought out bread and wine; now he was a priest of God Most High. 19 He blessed him and said, "Blessed be Abram of God Most High, Possessor of heaven and earth; 20 And blessed be God Most High, Who has delivered your enemies into your hand." He gave him a tenth of all.

THE ISSUE

Kevin Higgins writes: "Abraham's encounter with Melchizedek (a pagan priest of 'God Most High') shows us that the author of Genesis sees El and

Yahweh as the same Being. The fact that Abraham offers a tithe suggests an acceptance of the validity of Melchizedek's priesthood and thus, religion. This acceptance is confirmed by the New Testament view of Melchizedek as one of the crucial precursors of the Messiah. This is an astonishing acknowledgement of God's work in another religious tradition."[1]

In Other Words

Abraham knows Yahweh, but he meets Melchizedek who serves El (v.18). These names refer to the same God and this is confirmed by the New Testament's recognition that Melchizedek foreshadows Messiah. Therefore, Melchizedek's appearance and reality of his priesthood are evidence that God is at work in the religion of Melchizedek—and probably others as well.

MELCHIZEDEK

The conclusion about God "at work in another religious tradition" is funded by two observations: the two different names (El and Yahweh or to-*may*-to and to-*mah*-to) that refer to the one God; and the notion that Melchizedek is an antitype of Messiah. My concern is not Higgins' observations, but his conclusion. It is possible to make well-reasoned comments and observations but reach the wrong conclusion. For instance, in a study of one hundred recently deceased men and women, it was noted by the researchers that just prior to their deaths each one took a final breath, exhaled, and died. Researchers concluded breathing causes death.

Sometimes our observations do not necessarily lead to sound conclusions. Is God at work in another religious tradition in this story?

Melchizedek Who?

Melchizedek is an interesting person. One day he pops into the biblical narrative and as quickly as he appears, he vanishes. Where does he come from? Why is he important? What should we think about him?

First, his name is lightly disputed: it might mean "king of righteous [one?]" or "my king is righteous" while the writer of Hebrews calls him "king of righteousness" (7:2). His name appears twice in the Old Testament: Genesis 14 and Psalm 110:4. Regardless the precise meaning

---

1. Higgins, "Inside What?" 90.

of the name, the point is that although he is a person of interest, he is something of a mystery.

Melchizedek is What?

The second question to pursue is how we should understand his role: christophany, antitype of Messiah, simply an historical figure, or perhaps some combination?[2] The commentators have opinions covering the spectrum, so that's not a lot of help is it?

What Did Jesus Say about Melchizedek?

None of the gospel accounts show us Jesus uttering the name of Melchizedek, but Jesus did understand Psalm 110 as messianic, and it is here that Melchizedek's name is found. Jesus' priesthood is characterized in the Psalm in this manner: "You are a priest forever according to the order of Melchizedek" (v. 4). So Jesus understood that his own priesthood was eternal, after the order of Melchizedek. He would have understood this priesthood to be combined with kingship (as was Melchizedek's) and it would be unique in the sense that it was not Levitical, which was hereditary. It looks to me like Jesus knew Melchizedek was an historical figure who in some ways foreshadowed himself. But what about Melchizedek's religion?

The Religion of Melchizedek

We know Melchizedek was a priest, but that is all we really do know. Most of the rest is guesswork. Not having lots of information does not keep some proponents of IM from coming to the conclusion that God was at work in the religious tradition of Melchizedek. As I see it, the fact is this: Abraham offered a tithe to the priest, signifying Abraham accepted the religion—or at least Melchizedek—as valid. Therefore, God is at "work in

---

2. There are least two major theories as to Melchizedek's identification. The first can be summarized by understanding him as a human being of some sort: a) he was Shem or a son of Shem; b) or he was the son or grandson of Canaan; c) or he was, based on the book of Enoch, the son of Noah's deceased sister-in-law, making him a nephew to Noah. This latter story is more fun than the others since it has Melchizedek taken to heaven by an angel to escape the flood. When the waters receded, he returned as priest; but he shall also return at the end times. The second theory is that Melchizedek was the Cosmic Christ, a view held by Mark the Hermit of the fifth century, and others.

another religious tradition"? I agree with everything until we get to new tradition part.

Don't you wonder which religious tradition this was? If it was something in which God was working, it must have been an important religion, but Moses tells us very little about it. And if it was a tradition in which God was working, this could imply that Yahweh initiated the religion, making it an authentic, Yahweh-oriented religious tradition. Did it begin and end with Melchizedek? How did it develop? Furthermore, if it was a religious tradition in which God was working, why didn't Moses tell us that? Why the secret Moses? I certainly wonder about all this, but the matter is not explored by the advocates of IM. The *fact* of Melchizedek's religion is accepted at face value as an imponderable, I guess. Is there anything in the context of the story that might tip us off? I believe there is something in the wider context that might answer some of these questions.

Looking for Melchizedekism

The great man before the beginning of Abraham's story was Noah. When Noah disembarked from the ark, one of the first things he did was to offer up a sacrifice (Gen 8:20). Where did Noah learn to do this? Who taught him how to make a sacrifice? We don't really know, but we do know his sons were with him, and one in particular, Shem—the only son whose descendants are mentioned both before and after Babel (cf. Gen 11:1–9)—would have witnessed the sacrifice. The significance of Shem is that Abraham and Melchizedek were in the line of Shem (Gen 11:10–26). But the fact that both Noah and Shem knew about sacrifice begs the question: how is it that Noah knew about sacrifice?

If you continue to plunge backward into the storyline of Genesis, the great (to the seventh power) grandfather of Noah was Seth. After Seth fathered Enosh, Moses wrote, "Then men began to call upon the name of the Lord" (Gen 4:26). So I am guessing that Seth taught Enosh about sacrifice, who then taught his son, until the sacrifice was eventually taught to Noah and then Shem. From Shem it would finally reach Abraham. Seth learned about sacrifice from Adam, his father, whom I am supposing was taught directly by Yahweh.

So where am I going with all this? Remember the conclusion was that God is at "work in another religious tradition." Melchizedek is even called a "pagan priest." If all my supposing is correct, I must disagree with this conclusion. *Melchizedekism* is not just another religious tradition, and Melchizedek not just another pagan priest. This is quite possibly a tradition that Yahweh himself initiated. If this is true, Melchizedek is not a pagan and Yahweh is not at work inside *another* religious tradition, but inside his own. Robert Culver does not take the true worship of Yahweh back as far as I have pushed it, but he does say: "The appearance of Melchizedek in the Bible is important theologically. It lends strong support for the notion that knowledge of the true God possessed by Noah and his sons did not die out. . . . In the person of Melchizedek we find evidence of an ancient near eastern tradition of true worship at Jerusalem long before Ornan the Jebusite transferred title of the rocky 'Mount Moriah' to the crown."[3]

But What if I'm Wrong?

What do we really know about Melchizedek? He is a murky character who emerges out of the darkness of the past in order to play a small role in God's discipleship of Abraham. That much we know. What do we really know about his religion? We know he was a priest. We don't know that he sacrificed—that was, of course, an assumption on my part. We don't know anything about the rituals he performed as a priest. Therefore, if this is all we really know about Melchizedek, proponents of IM are reading far too much into the scripture to use Melchizedek as an adherent of a religion in which Yahweh is working. My own example of tracing sacrifice back to Yahweh to show Melchizedek's religion was not pagan but Yahweh-initiated is just as tenuous. We just don't have enough information about Melchizedek to warrant Higgins' conclusion.

ALTAR-NATE ENDING?

The topic of religion raises one more interesting question in the story of Melchizedek. What religion did Abraham belong to? We know he had a relationship with Yahweh, though we don't know the particulars of any religious rites he may have performed other than a few sacrifices and that he built altars. We certainly know Abraham was not Jewish. It is ironic that on the one hand we are told that Melchizedek was part of another religion—though I have argued his religious tradition was not "another," but begun by God himself—while on the other hand the protagonist of

3. Culver, "Melchizedek," 510.

the story, Abraham, had a confirmed relationship with the Almighty without any religion ever being mentioned.

So in the case of Melchizedek, I am guessing that Yahweh was working in his own created religious tradition, while in the situation with Abraham, God chose to meet him personally without the help of any religious tradition; however, when we think seriously about the entire story of Melchizedek and Abraham, the uniqueness of the story is what must be emphasized. The story is not some type of parallel connection from the eighteenth century BC to the twenty-first century in our work among Muslims. The story stands uniquely as an indication that Yahweh has been working throughout history to call out a people for himself so that through them, the Jews I mean, he would eventually send his son as the Redeemer for all those ensnared in the false religions of our own making.

4

Second Kings 5, Rimmon-iscing

Naaman the Syrian, a soldier of some repute, was healed of leprosy during the ministry of Elisha when he washed himself in the Jordan. As a result of the miraculous healing, Naaman returned to his master a new man, a transformed man. But what interests us is his conversation with Elisha before Naaman left for home.

SECOND KINGS 5:15-19

15 When he *[Naaman]* returned to the man of God *[Elisha]* with all his company, and came and stood before him, he said, "Behold now, I know that there is no God in all the earth, but in Israel; so please take a present from your servant now." 16 But he said, "As the LORD lives, before whom I stand, I will take nothing." And he urged him to take *it*, but he refused. 17 Naaman said, "If not, please let your servant at least be given two mules' load of earth; for your servant will no longer offer burnt offering nor will he sacrifice to other gods, but to the LORD. 18 In this matter may the LORD pardon your servant: when my master goes into the house of Rimmon to worship there, and he leans on my hand and I bow myself in the house of Rimmon, when I bow myself in the house of Rimmon, the LORD pardon your servant in this matter." 19 He said to him, "Go in peace." So he departed from him some distance.

THE ISSUE

Kevin Higgins writes,

Naaman clearly changes at least some of his beliefs. He now acknowledges that there is no God in all the earth except "in Israel" (v. 15). Yet, some of his old ways of thinking remain: since there is no God except in Israel, he asks for some of Israel's dirt that he might take it with him to Aram (v. 17). The Prophet allows him to remain in this belief about the connection between the dirt of Israel and the God of Israel. The process of change in an insider's belief system will be a dynamic one. However, there is a clear and fundamental change of Naaman's belief about God.[1]

IN OTHER WORDS

Naaman, healed of leprosy through Elisha, remained inside his religion even though he believed Yahweh was the one true God. This is an example of God calling someone to himself and the believer staying in his religion.

DO WE KNOW WHAT WE DON'T KNOW?

What really happened to Naaman; what are the facts? First, he made a genuine confession: "I know that there is no God in all the earth, but in Israel." This seems an admission that he not only believed in Yahweh, but he was also renouncing Rimmon (remember this *turning to* and *turning from* business; it will prove important in Chapter 11). Second, Elisha did not comment on the notion that Naaman needed Israeli soil for worship. Third, Naaman asked about the necessity of accompanying his master when the latter worships the god Rimmon. The implication is that while the master is bowing, Naaman will be helping him to accomplish the worship, but Naaman himself would not perform the worship. Fourth, Elisha said, "Go in peace." This is hardly a stamp of approval on what Naaman was about to do. In fact, it seems hard to draw a firm conclusion from the facts about Elisha and Naaman.

Still the question immediately jumps out at me: was the nature of Naaman's request for permission or forgiveness? Was he saying something like this: "Elisha, when I am in the temple of Rimmon with my master, is it alright to bow in worship to Rimmon as my master bows?" Or was he asking, "Elisha, even when I need to help my master bow, you know of course I am not bowing to Rimmon. Is this forgivable?" Tennent speaks to this point: "The one thing we *do* know is that the context of the passage

---

1. Higgins, "Inside What?" 90.

Second Kings 5, Rimmon-iscing 27

is about Naaman asking for *forgiveness* for doing something which they both knew was wrong, not the Prophet's *blessing* for promoting any activity or strategy or self-identity of Naaman as a follower of Rimmon."[2]

I tend to agree with Tennent on this, but even if Naaman were asking for permission, it doesn't change the fact that both Elisha and Naaman knew that worshipping Rimmon—especially now that Naaman was a changed man—was wrong. How is this parallel to what is happening to followers of Jesus who stay inside Islam? These insiders believe they are doing something right, even noble. They are remaining inside the religion that brought them into the world unlike Naaman, who was contrite, recognizing it was wrong to worship Rimmon.

Consider insider Mazhar Mallouhi's comments on being an insider: "I was born into a confessional home. Islam is the blanket with which my mother wrapped me up when she nursed me and sang to me and prayed over me. I imbibed aspects of Islam with my mother's milk. I inherited Islam from my parents and it was the cradle, which held me until I found Christ. Islam is my mother. You don't engage a person by telling them their mother is ugly."[3]

I agree with Mallouhi that the worst way to begin a relationship with him is to call his *mother* ugly, but if Mallouhi were to ask me what I think about this mother, I would encourage him to reconsider who his real parent is with something like this: "You have new parents. You have been adopted into a new family because your mother has disowned you. You now have a father! And he loves you enough to call you his son. Did your mother ever call you son or were you just her slave?"

SHH! SILENCE IS ARGUING

Whereas Naaman knew he should no longer go into the temple to worship Rimmon, his occupation required him to. This is in no way parallel to the insider position. Naaman was compelled to do something that he knew would appear to observers as worship, but his appeal was for forgiveness or perhaps even compassion or understanding, not blessing. Insiders, we are told by the proponents of IM, are not compelled to remain inside Islam and they are doing nothing wrong by doing so.

---

2. Tennent, "Followers," 108.
3. Mallouhi, "Comments," 8.

The story of Naaman does not help the insider movements' argument. There is too much that is different; the parallel to the situation with Muslims is not present. There is too much of an argument from silence, and too much that is questionable or ambiguous to find solid support for IM here.

5

Jonah 1, Nineveh Your Business

THERE'S NOTHING LIKE A good ocean storm to put the fear of God into a person. In the story of Jonah's attempted escape from Yahweh, we see a slightly salty slew of saintly sailors who, despite their paganism and crusty exterior, apparently had some type of relationship with Yahweh proving to be softies for God after all.

JONAH 1:14-17

14 Then they called on the LORD and said, "We earnestly pray, O LORD, do not let us perish on account of this man's life and do not put innocent blood on us; for You, O LORD, have done as You have pleased." 15 So they picked up Jonah, threw him into the sea, and the sea stopped its raging. 16 Then the men feared the LORD greatly, and they offered a sacrifice to the LORD and made vows. 17 And the LORD appointed a great fish to swallow Jonah, and Jonah was in the stomach of the fish three days and three nights.

THE ISSUE

Kevin Higgins is the only one of the advocates to use Jonah's story as an example for insider movements. He writes: "In the book of Jonah it is ironically not the Hebrew Jonah who hears and obeys God. In addition, it is the pagan sailors' prayers that are heard by Yahweh. When they cast lots, it is Yahweh who directs the answer. They are in relationship with Yahweh."[1]

IN OTHER WORDS

Because Yahweh heard the prayers of these pagan sailors, this is evidence of a relationship with Yahweh while still being adherents of another religion.

ARE YOU IN A RELATIONSHIP?

I think it's interesting the manner in which Higgins portrays the relationship of Yahweh and the pagans: "it is not . . . Jonah who hears and obeys God." Having said that, I would have expected to read this: "but it was the pagans who heard and obeyed God." However, that is not what was said. Instead of emphasizing the obedience of the pagans or the listening to God, the focus is upon Yahweh's hearing their prayers. Isn't this moving the goalposts of what a relationship is? For the Hebrew, relationship—covenant relationship—was understood through the lens of obedience, but here relationship with Yahweh for pagans is simply having one's prayers heard.

I've noticed how often we evangelicals throw around the word *relationship*. For us knowing Jesus is all about relationship—and rightly so. We wrinkle our nose at the question, "So what religion are you?" Visibly shaken with disgust we answer, "I don't have a religion. I have a relationship with Jesus." We have an evangelical knee-jerk reaction to hearing our relationship with Jesus described as a religion. We are disciples, followers, apprentices, Christians, and we are in relationship to Christ. Don't get me wrong. I have a relationship with Jesus, too. I'm only pointing out how we blithely use the word when it really means more than just, well, you know, a relationship.

I suspect this is what's going on with some of the advocates of insider movements. There is an overemphasis upon the *relationship* one might have with Yahweh, especially if one is a pagan. We've seen it with Melchizedek (a non-Jew whose religion was unknown, though possibly initiated by Yahweh), with Naaman (a non-Jew who believed in Yahweh and knew worshiping Rimmon was wrong), and now with the pagan

---

1. Higgins, "Inside What?" 85.

sailors manning Jonah's sinking ship. When someone tells us they have a relationship with Yahweh, our evangelical brains melt into a lukewarm mound of mush. The magic word *relationship* has been used and we often don't go farther than that. But why should we think the pagan sailors had any kind of relationship with Yahweh?

It is alleged that the pagan sailors had relationship with Yahweh based on the answer they received to their prayers for deliverance; therefore, *ergo hoc ad propter* (the cool Latin way to say, *voila*, which is the cool French way to say the boring English, "Will you look at that!"): *relationship*! Let's look at the story more closely.

WHO REALLY HAS THE RELATIONSHIP TO YAHWEH?

"The word of the Lord came to Jonah" (1:1). Yahweh spoke to Jonah and gave him a message: "Arise, go to Nineveh" (1:2). We all know he didn't go to Nineveh; rather he pulled a one-eighty and set off for Tarshish (1:3).

So, Jonah was fleeing God's direct command. He was probably feeling pretty good about how he got out of town without the Creator of the universe knowing about it (I wrote that with some satirical delight). Notice the author tells us Jonah was escaping "from the presence of the Lord." It would be impossible for Jonah to escape from something he had never experienced. I know that I flee with great haste when I see tomatoes because I know how they taste. If I'd never personally experienced a tomato, why would I run away? The same is true for Jonah: he had experience with Yahweh as his God.

Let me recap what's happened up to this point. God spoke to Jonah giving him a directive. Jonah refused and attempted to wriggle out from God's presence like a worm trapped by a bird. Jonah tried to escape from God's face. That's a pretty intimate kind of relationship don't you think? And why did Jonah disobey a direct order from his God? We are not told in chapter one, but later Jonah said, "I knew that Thou art a gracious and compassionate God, slow to anger and abundant in lovingkindness, and One who relents concerning calamity" (4:2). Jonah knew Yahweh so well—that means he had a relationship with him—he understood that if he preached against Nineveh, God would have compassion on the reprobates rather than sending the death ray. And what kind of a prophet would Jonah have been if he couldn't get God to pull the trigger on these ne'er-do-wells?

Are you beginning to see the depth of Jonah's knowledge about and relationship with Yahweh? What did the pagans know about God? We're not told; but Jonah had a past with Yahweh. He knew him. He had experiences with his God. In fact, Jonah had a real relationship with him.

PRAYER IN A FOXHOLE

For now let's forget that Jonah is the one who had the verifiable relationship with Yahweh. The pagan sailors prayed, Yahweh heard their prayers, and so we have the evidence that those inside another religion can have a walk with the Lord. Is that what really took place?

Let's get a little more context under our belts before we decide whether Higgins is right or not. As a result of Jonah's disobedience, God sent a storm (1:4). The storm did not come because the sailors were in a covenant relationship to Yahweh whom they were disobeying, but because Jonah was. Jonah's relationship caused God to go after him with a big stick. As a father, I don't go around disciplining everyone else's children, much as I might like to; but I certainly discipline my own children. Why? The *R-word*: relationship.

Naturally the sailors grew alarmed at the intensity of the storm; they feared for their lives (1:5–6). They did everything their experience with storms taught them, but nothing was working. They were close to being swamped and ending up in Dawud Jones' locker. So one of the sailors, probably the one who believed in the pagan art of divining by reading goat innards, pulled out his trusty lots-for-travelers from its waterproof carrying-case (1:7). I'm fairly certain the slogan on the case read, "If you're tired of entrails, Lots-in-a-Box will give you the details." And casting the lot, wouldn't you know it, it fell to Jonah. Jonah was in lots of trouble now. Isn't it interesting that the lot fell upon the one in relationship with Yahweh, not on any of the pagan sailors?

After some more handwringing and sending a few more urns of olive oil into the briny deep—possibly creating the Mediterranean's first real oil spill—the crew was left with one choice: prayer to Yahweh. "O Lord, do not let us perish on account of this man's life and do not put innocent blood on us; for Thou, O Lord, has done as Thou hast pleased" (1:14). Before the one praying could utter amen, the sailors rudely threw Jonah overboard and the Lord sent a large fish to swallow him (1:15).

Whose prayer did Yahweh answer? It would seem it was the sailors' prayer, but there is something I deliberately did not mention in the narrative. In Jonah 1:6 we are told the captain roused Jonah from sleep and demanded he pray to his god. We may surmise this is what Jonah did. He prayed. Of course this is only an inference from the story, so I don't want to rest on it as solid evidence.[2] Let's return to the prayer of the sailors.

Yes, they prayed; it was an eloquent, heart-felt prayer of a single syllable: "Help!" But because Yahweh apparently answered the pagans' prayer, does this prove there is a relationship between them? And what is the nature of that relationship when the prayer is offered in desperation, from a foxhole (or the bird's nest)? Really the question I'm asking is this: what is the basis upon which Yahweh answers prayers? Is it from his own character and will that prayers are answered; or are answered prayers dependent upon the relationship between the Lord and the one who prays?

ANSWERED PRAYERS

Is there a principle of answered prayer, for why and for whom God answers prayers? Psalm 143:1 says, "Hear my prayer, O Lord, give ear to my supplications! Answer me in Thy faithfulness, in Thy righteousness!" Notice the emphasis on the character of God, not the quality of the relationship between David and Yahweh. For similar passages, consider Psalm 4:1 (he answers out of his graciousness), and Psalm 69:13 (he answers out of his love). But a passage that perhaps gives greater insight into answered prayer is Psalm 86:1–10, especially verse 5: "For Thou, Lord, art good, and ready to forgive, and abundant in lovingkindness to all who call upon Thee."

From David we learn that the real basis for answered prayer is the very character of God: he is good; he is ready to forgive; he is full of overflowing love. David seems to say, "Just ask." Love, of course, is part of a relationship, but in this case it is God's love for us, the pray-*ers*, not our love for God. The relationship may be mutual; that is, the petitioner may love God too, but nothing about answered prayer demands it. The direction of the relationship is really unidirectional: from God to man; from the one who answers prayers to the one who prays.

---

2. It's also quite likely that Jonah did not pray at all. After all, he was trying to get away from God and would not have been tempted to enter into prayer with his persecutor.

Answered prayer comes about because of the will and character of our God. When we are told the pagan sailors were in relationship to Yahweh, this is right, of course, at some level. The problem is that the depth, level, and quality of the relationship is not explained or explored. Higgins just drops the *R-bomb* on the evangelical audience setting off a chain reaction in our twenty-first century minds: "Oh! These pagans have a relationship to Yahweh. So do I. How wonderful!"

Whatever relationship the pagan sailors had with Yahweh did not ultimately matter in the story. God certainly heard them pray, as he hears all prayers—how can he not since we put up so many so often—but that he responded to the prayer was not necessarily dependent upon any level or depth of maturity in the sailor's relationship with Yahweh. Answered prayer is dependent upon the overabundance of love, compassion, and good will of our Father.

What of the New Testament? Does it agree with the Old Testament? I don't believe Jesus changed this essential picture of prayer, but he did add some interesting nuances. For instance, on several occasions Jesus healed the sick at the request of one to whom he said, "Your faith has made you well" (Matt 9:22); and other time, "Oh woman, your faith is great; be it done for you as you wish" (Matt 15:28); and in a parable about prayer Jesus had a character say, "because the widow bothers me, I will give her legal protection, lest by continually coming she wear me out" (Luke 18:5), thus teaching us to keep on praying. On the other hand, many times Jesus answered requests when moved with compassion (Matt 20:34; Mark 1:41; Luke 7:13). So in the life of Jesus we see both occasions for answered prayer: the faith and persistence of the one asking and his own compassion.

BRINGING THE SHIP HOME

How do we put all this together as it relates to the pagan sailors in Jonah 1? First, it overreaches the story to baldly state the sailors "are in relationship with Yahweh" with so little explanation and exploration of what that means. I have attempted to show that *relationship*—the way we misunderstand it—can mean anything from a foxhole prayer to the intimate and personal closeness of a prophet like Jonah who has experienced God's character. Surely the suggestion is not that the pagan sailors had the same quality of relationship that Jonah shared? But that's what is implied when we are told these sailors have their prayer answered. And second, I have emphasized that answered prayer is not necessarily dependent upon one's relationship to God—or the lack of relationship—but upon the character and goodness of God himself. There is certainly an element of faith and persistence in some answered requests, but in each case we are told *that* is why the answer was given. If answered prayer were the measure of being in relationship with Yahweh, it would necessitate saying that anyone who has ever called out to God for anything—for rain, for luck at poker, for a parking space at the mall during Christmas time—means that person is intimately in love with God. But in the case of the sailors of Jonah 1, we are not told of their faith or persistence. We only see the compassion of Yahweh. To use the example of the pagan sailor's experience with prayer as evidence of a relationship while in another religion is to row a boat with many holes.

6

John 4 and Acts 8, The Sounds of Silence

THE SAMARITANS WERE CERTAINLY a different religion from the Jews, yet Yahweh was working within the Samaritan culture and religion. Some proponents of insider movements believe the two occasions of Samaritan conversions in John and Acts support the notion of Yahweh at work within another religion, and further show us that Yahweh does not ask a person to leave his culture in order to become a believer.

JOHN 4:39–43

39 From that city many of the Samaritans believed in Him because of the word of the woman who testified, "He told me all the things that I have done." 40 So when the Samaritans came to Jesus, they were asking Him to stay with them; and He stayed there two days. 41 Many more believed because of His word; 42 and they were saying to the woman, "It is no longer because of what you said that we believe, for we have heard for ourselves and know that this One is indeed the Savior of the world." 43 After the two days He went forth from there into Galilee.

ACTS 8:14–17

14 Now when the apostles in Jerusalem heard that Samaria had received the word of God, they sent them Peter and John, 15 who came down and prayed for them that they might receive the Holy Spirit. 16 For He had not yet fallen upon any of them; they had simply been baptized in the

name of the Lord Jesus. 17 Then they began laying their hands on them, and they were receiving the Holy Spirit.

THE ISSUE

John 4

Rebecca Lewis rightly points out one of the major concerns of the story from John 4: "Jesus Himself had previously affirmed to the Samaritan woman, and later to her whole town, that true faith is not limited to Jewish religious forms, but consists in worshipping God in spirit and in truth."[1]

Kevin Higgins sees a bit more in the story: "After their conversion recorded in John 4, they worshipped in spirit and in truth. But they did so in Samaria (in their prior place of worship) just as Jesus worshipped the Father in spirit and in truth in Jerusalem, in the Temple. A second feature of the passage further suggests that this episode is an example of an Insider Movement. After Jesus spends two days in the Samaritan village, the villagers affirm that they now believe Jesus is the Savior of the world. Then Jesus leaves. What does He leave behind? A group of believers."[2]

Acts 8

Again, Lewis writes about the Samaritan condition: "Later in Acts we see that Samaritan believers remained in their own communities and retained their Samaritan identity. But at first the disciples did not understand that just as they could remain Jews and follow Jesus, the Samaritans could also remain Samaritan."[3]

Stuart Caldwell, executive director of Global Teams, a missionary sending organization based in California, asks an interesting question: "Why don't we see the Apostles extracting believers out of Samaritanism?"[4]

IN OTHER WORDS

The fact that Samaritans became followers of Jesus while remaining Samaritans is a model for Muslims who follow Jesus, but remain within Islam.

1. Lewis, "Promoting," 76.
2. Higgins, "The Key," 159.
3. Lewis, "Insider," 17.
4. Caldwell, "Jesus in Samaria," 26.

A CLOSER LOOK JOHN 4

Simply stated, each of the three proponents of IM argues from what is *not* said. Before a conclusion is drawn about what the two stories do teach us, let's look at the facts and see what they do and do not tell us about the Samaritans.

First in Jesus' conversation with the woman at the well, it is indeed a fact that the Samaritans worshipped in Samaria, but Jesus, as a Jew, worshipped in Jerusalem. The Samaritans did experience a conversion, but stayed culturally Samaritans. This is the first claim as evidence for an insider movement: Samaritans were not required to worship in Jerusalem.

I find it interesting that the woman says in verse 20, "But you say that in Jerusalem is the place where people ought to worship." Jesus never said this; at least John does not record it. It seems reasonable for the woman to believe this of Jesus; he was a Jew and Jews believed worship in the temple was significant. So she was simply repeating a generalization about what the Jews believed. But what John does record is Jesus saying, "The Father is seeking such people to worship him. God is spirit, and those who worship him must worship in spirit and truth" (4:23–24). Apparently, neither the Jew nor the Samaritan had it completely right. That is to say, true worship does not require a special place, but an attitude and proper relationship as a child to his or her father. Of course Jesus would not require the Samaritans to go to Jerusalem for worship. Why would he? He wasn't requiring it for Jews in this statement. But is this an evidence of an insider movement?

The second fact is related to the first: John says absolutely nothing about what Samaritan belief looked like in John 4. Did the Samaritans continue to perform sacrifices or did they stop? Did they continue to read the Samaritan Torah or did they trot off to Barnes and Goldberg for a real *Tanakh*? Did they sack all their priests and anoint new ones? Did they become Jews? I know the advocates of the IM would say, "No! They remained Samaritans." But I would remind you that we simply don't know. We don't know if they became Jews, Samaritan Jews, Jewish Samaritans, completed Samaritans, Messianic Samaritanical Jews, or Christians. John tells us nothing. So how do we know the Samaritans provide evidence of an insider movement? We don't. We don't know because we cannot know—the second fact.

Here's the third fact from John 4: Jesus did spend two days with the Samaritans. We also know that "many more believed because of his word" (4:41). What is John's conclusion about this intensive two-day stopover by Jesus? "He departed for Galilee" (4:43). He left. What did he leave behind? He left behind a group of believers, of course (fact three). That's all we know.

So we know three things from John 4: first, there were Samaritan conversions; second, we have no idea what that looked like (that is, if they worshipped as Samaritan followers of Jesus, as Jews, or something completely different); and third, when Jesus departed he left behind believers. How can one build a case for an insider movement from the text unless the reader brings the idea to the text? Eisegesis makes for great speculation, but offers a pretty shaky foundation.

ACTS 8

As with John 4, let me offer the facts before coming to a conclusion. First we know the Samaritans listened to Philip's preaching and accepted it with "much rejoicing in the city" (8:8). It looks like the evidence of their conversion was the joy they experienced.

But Luke says nothing about identity, culture, Samaritan values or society, and nothing about the Samaritan religion except for the implication they *turned from* their religion (dare I say *from* their socio-religious structure?) when they *turned to* Christ. This implication I take to be part of the joy they expressed at conversion. Many of us understand the burden of oppressive religions since we've come to Christ. Jesus takes away our guilt, shame and powerlessness because of sin and makes us free to serve him. Jesus removes the burden of having to be good enough, holy enough, and faithful enough in our rituals to please God. But again, I ask, what in the story tells us the Samaritans remained in their socio-religious forms of ritual and worship?

The second relevant fact from this story is found in verse 25. Peter and Philip continued on through other Samaritan villages preaching the gospel. Luke mentioned nothing about whether or not these new villages accepted the message. He does not tell us what Samaritan believers looked like, what they did, how they worshipped, and how they organized. Luke remains silent on this subject.

SAMARITAN EXTRACT

Caldwell asks, "Why don't we see the Apostles extracting believers out of Samaritanism?" My initial reaction is, "Why doesn't Luke say why the Apostles *are not extracting* the Samaritans?" This is an argument from silence. Besides, it was not an issue for Luke, but it is an issue the proponents of IM bring to the text. Luke didn't raise the matter because it didn't matter. The question doesn't fit the context of the story. What in the story makes us think extraction was an issue?

Normal Extraction?

One of the realities of Muslim ministry—not ministry among Samaritans—is extraction. The typical scenario for a new convert's discipleship is to see him extracted from or become irrelevant to his culture. In other words, the new convert begins to adopt the lifestyle and manners of the discipler, the missionary. If the missionary is Western, eventually the convert is discipled to be a Western Christian. I have oversimplified this, but you get the idea. It is generally believed that the extraction model has been the historical norm among missions to Muslims. This is the first type of extraction.

Apostate Extraction

But what is often overlooked is that Islam itself pushes out those who are apostates. The second form of extraction comes from Islam itself. The doctrine of Islam is very clear: the one who leaves Islam is given time to repent and return to the religion. If the apostate refuses, he must be put to death. Now whether or not the punishment actually takes place—and it is far less commonly carried out than one might think—the apostate is under penalty of death.[5] It could be argued therefore, extraction from Islam may be more an effect of Islam itself rather than an event caused by the missionary.[6]

---

5. There is some discussion going on among Muslims about the death penalty for apostates. The "let Allah revenge" crowd, led by Indian-born Muslim Zakir Naik, argues there is no death penalty for apostasy. This is based on the hadith from Ahmad 3.4345. The traditional argument, "let's kill the apostate," is based on Q4:137 and al Bukhari vo. 9, bk. 83, no. 17 and argues the hadith of al Bukhari trumps the Ahmad hadith. Therefore apostates must be killed. Many who believe the latter are careful not to carry out the letter of the law if the Muslim community is the minority and without power in their society.

6. I am obliged to Fred Farrokh, executive director of *Jesus for Muslims* (www.jesus-

Jesus' Type of Extraction

Now put Jesus into the Samaritan context of Acts 8. The proponents of IM would have us believe, despite the lack of confirmation in either John 4 or Acts 8, that the Samaritans were not extracted from the Samaritan culture. They were not made into non-Samaritans by the discipleship and teaching Jesus gave. On the face of it, you might think it foolish to disagree. You might be surprised to know I don't; that is I don't want to be foolish. Neither Lewis nor Caldwell give us any specifics as to what Jesus' discipleship 101 class looked like among the Samaritans. Did he teach them to be faithful Samaritans and to love Yahweh? Did he teach them to go up to Jerusalem? Maybe he taught them to play soccer. We don't know. Luke doesn't tell us anything about what Jesus taught them.

I guess we could say Jesus did not extract the Samaritans from their culture, but we can only say it on the basis of our hopes, not on the basis of the text. I do believe Jesus did not extract the Samaritans from their culture in order to make them Jews. But hoping doesn't make it true. I am even willing to say that for Jesus to tell the Samaritans to stop being Samaritans would go against his own nature. But if I tell you this is what the text says I would be inventing something out of thin air. To properly understand scripture, we have to let it speak; we cannot speak into it what we hope to hear.

Extraction is an interesting concept to which I think most advocates of insider movements do not give enough thought. Extraction is a much more complicated phenomenon that simply finding oneself no longer relevant to one's culture thanks to some Western missionary.

Jesus demanded extraction; I believe this is the third type of extraction. That should be like a punch in the stomach! He called for self-extraction. That's right. Jesus demanded self-extraction, but that doesn't mean the believer becomes irrelevant to his family, his culture or society. Ostracism—the main feature that Jesus seemed to mention—is not irrelevance, but is in fact, the confrontation of the gospel with the culture. Consider these passages and their implications:

- "Blessed are you when men hate you, and ostracize you, and insult you, and scorn your name as evil, for the sake of the Son of Man" (Luke 6:22).

---

formuslims.org) for this observation.

- Loving Jesus means facing the possibility of ostracism. This can come from the larger society, but more than likely, it will come from the believer's family. Separation, at least in some cases, is the norm. This may not be extraction (where a neutral party removes the victim), but the result is the same.

- "If anyone wishes to come after Me, he must deny himself, and take up his cross daily and follow Me" (Luke 9:23).
  - Self-extraction, perhaps not from society or one's family, but from "the world" is the result of a close, intimate walk with Jesus. Following Jesus must surely result in separation from one's culture and "the world." Again, this seems to be expected, the norm, and not the exception.

- "If anyone comes to Me, and does not hate his own father and mother and wife and children and brothers and sisters, yes, and even his own life, he cannot be My disciple" (Luke 14:26).
  - There is an inherent separation that exists between believers and non-believers even in the same family. Our love for Jesus should exceed our love for any family member, which could certainly be misunderstood by our loved ones.

I am not suggesting the model of removing a convert from his family must be done as if he were a noxious weed in a flowerbed, but it is short-sighted to think all extraction for just any reason is missionary policy. I also do not want to suggest that our mission methods of the past are beyond reproach. There were many mistakes, as there are mistakes being made today, but we should also acknowledge the tremendous debt we owe to our missionary forebears. So, when we are told the Apostles were not extracting the Samaritans—even though it is an argument from silence—we should not immediately jump to the conclusion that extraction is wrong or a poorly thought-out strategy. It may be an appropriate, scripturally directed action.

Ultimately, our exegesis of the scriptures must not be built on silence. Are we exegeting scripture because of what we deem to be logical, sociologically permissible, or perhaps jumping to inferences from silence, then leaping to conclusions from our inferences? Or does our exegesis allow scripture to say what it says? It is only when we let scripture speak that we can offer appropriate inferences for application. The example of the Samaritans in John 4 and Acts 8 offers insider movements nothing but the hush of silence. Can you hear the crickets?

7

Acts 15, Parallel Universe?

Is the situation of Muslims coming to Christ while remaining within their God-given networks parallel in the book of Acts to the gentiles coming to Christ while remaining gentiles? The advocates of IM believe so.

ACTS 15:19–21

19 Therefore it is my judgment that we do not trouble those who are turning to God from among the gentiles, 20 but that we write to them that they abstain from things contaminated by idols and from fornication and from what is strangled and from blood. 21 For Moses from ancient generations has in every city those who preach him, since he is read in the synagogues every Sabbath.

THE ISSUE

Rebecca Lewis understands the passage in terms of the methodology we can learn:

> First, they heard that the Holy Spirit had descended on believers from a pagan background who were not practicing the Jewish religion. Second, they realized the scriptures had predicted that this would happen. These two criteria were sufficient for the apostles to conclude that God was behind this new movement of believers who were remaining gentile. Therefore, they did not oppose it or add on demands for religious conversion. *If we use the same two criteria today,* insider movements affirm that people do not even

have to go through the religion of Christianity, but only through Jesus Christ, to enter God's family[1] (emphasis mine).

IN OTHER WORDS

Followers of Jesus from a Muslim background today face a similar situation as the gentiles of Acts 15; and using Acts 15's criteria, we can help new believers enter the kingdom through Jesus rather than through Christianity.

ACTS-CESSING THE FIRST CRITERION

Of all the passages cited as foundational to expressing the biblical teaching for insider movements, Acts 15 is the most complex.[2] So we want be sure we understand the context and what was really going on in Jerusalem.

The advocates of IM offer up as the most important element of the story: salvation. I agree; this is the focus. Higgins writes, "Peter's conclusion in verse 11 makes it clear that the question is soteriological in nature."[3] The question concerned the gentiles and the law. Was it necessary for the gentiles to keep the law of Moses in order to be saved? The answer given by the Jerusalem council led by James, the brother of Jesus, was a resounding, "No."

ACTS-PERIENCE MEASURED BY THE WORD OF GOD

A second issue of importance is that various reports were given during the council's meeting. First to speak were the Judaizers (v. 5), followed by Peter (vv. 7ff), then Barnabas and Paul (v. 12), followed by James' resolution on behalf of the council (vv. 13ff). These reports confirmed that God gave the gentiles the same Holy Spirit he sent on the day of Pentecost (v. 8).

---

1. Lewis, "Insider Movements," 18.

2. I am indebted to Doug Coleman for the general direction I take on Acts 15 (D. Coleman, "A Theological Analysis of the Insider Movement Paradigm from Four Perspectives: Theology of Religions, Revelation, Soteriology, and Ecclesiology." PhD Dissertation, Southeastern Baptist Theological Seminary, May 2011).

3. Higgins, "Acts 15," 30. See Marshall who writes: "Luke's account of the discussion regarding the relation of the gentiles to the law of Moses forms the center of Acts both structurally and theologically" (Marshall, *The Acts of the Apostles*, 242).

According to Lewis the reports coming from missionaries on the field today—from Bangladesh, India, Indonesia, and elsewhere—are parallel to the reports given in Acts 15. They are recording the move of God among Muslims just as Peter, Barnabas and Paul announced the move of God among the gentiles. Lewis writes:

> I believe one of the most instructive aspects of Acts 15 is not their conclusions, but the process they followed. They looked at what God had been doing. . . . They respected the fact that God "who knows the heart showed that he accepted them by giving the Holy Spirit to them just as he did to us" (Acts 15:8). They listened carefully to the case studies of Paul and Barnabas (vs. 12). They noted that the scriptures pointed to the fact that God would redeem people from the gentiles (vs. 17). Then they concluded they should not make it difficult for other people to turn to God (vs. 19). *We can follow the same careful process they modeled.* It was the Pharisee believers (vs. 5) who did not want to actually look at what God was doing but stand on the Law of Moses as a matter of principle.[4] (emphasis mine)

I concur; I too believe our observations are important when considering God's activities, but these observations must be measured against the Word of God—and this must be done correctly. I could claim God is a chicken based on Psalm 36:7 ("and the children of men take refuge in the shadow of your wings"). Lewis encourages us to use the same processes found in Acts 15 when judging what God is doing today. I agree that the process of observation, comparison with scripture, and debate is important. After all that's what we are doing in this book. So we agree on these two premises: the issue is salvation and the process is important.

---

4. Lewis cited in Gary Corwin, "A Humble Appeal,"11. In a separate article, Dick Brogden writes, "Insider movements are the current creative missiological rage." Lewis responds to Brogden: "This statement implies missiologists invented 'insider movements' and are promoting them as a new technique. In fact, these type of movements started to happen and *we are being forced to evaluate if they are biblically legitimate.* When Paul and Peter stood before the Jerusalem council, they were reacting to events, not introducing a new 'creative missiological' approach to the gentiles. They were asking 'If God is accepting these people by giving them the Holy Spirit, what should our response be?' We are forced by events to ask similar questions today" (Brogden, "Inside Out," 33; emphasis mine). My point is to show, again, the importance of field reports to the substantiation of insider movements.

Unexamined Parallelism Investigated

Lewis believes there is a parallelism between the Acts 15 situation and the movement to Jesus among Muslims today.[5] But she posits the parallelism without further explanation or substantiation with the scripture she believes suggests it.

In the quote at the beginning of this chapter she argues there is a process at work in Acts 15: first, the reality of God coming into the lives of the gentiles as witnessed by the missionaries; and second, this is measured or confirmed by the statements of scripture. The conclusion is that the same thing is happening today among Muslims. But is it?

To begin the investigation into the assumption of God's parallel activity, I have synthesized the two criteria (Table 2). The first criterion, gentiles coming to faith, is indeed parallel to Muslims coming to faith as confirmed by missionary observation. The same Spirit given to us is falling on Muslims. No one doubts this, though when it comes to the incredible reports coming out of Bangladesh and Ethiopia, let me just say, I always put on my hat that says, *You're kidding, right?* The second criterion is where our disagreement is found. Lewis believes Acts 15 parallels today because the scriptures supported the missionary observations of the first century as they support what is happening in the insider movements today.

Table 2. The two criteria for judging the insider movements parallel to Acts 15.

Criteria in Acts 15	Criteria Today	Verification
Gentiles coming to faith	Muslims coming to faith	Missionary observation
Amos 9:11–12; Jer 12:15; Is 45:21	Gen 14; 2 Kgs 5; Jonah 1; Jn 4; Acts 8 and 15	Proper understanding of scripture

Each of the passages—Gen 14, 2 Kgs 5, Jonah 1, and John and Acts and the others—do not support Lewis' second criterion. Either the argument comes from silence, relies on the ambiguity of the story, or derives its significance eisegetically. The same is true for this passage as well. Let's test the supposed parallelism.

---

5. Upon reading this chapter, Lewis wished to make clear that she does not believe Judaism and Islam are parallel; however, what I'm arguing here is that she sees the two situations—the first century and today—as parallel.

Three Exams

The First

The first century situation is parallel to the Muslims coming to faith in one of three main areas. The gentiles were saved without being circumcised, that is, by not going through Judaism. This is correct. It is a parallel situation for the Muslims today—in fact a parallel situation for all people coming to Jesus. Jesus saves them; Christianity does not.

Let's not mix up two important ideas though. The Bible says that we are saved by grace through faith (Eph 2:8-9); and that our faith is placed in Jesus. Nowhere are we told to place our trust in Christianity. The statement that "we are not saved by Christianity" offered up by many advocates of IM, deflects us from realizing that when we place our faith in Jesus, the result is that we become Christians. It is true we do not go through the experience of becoming a Christian in order to follow Jesus, but it is also true that our faith in Christ does make us Christians. So as we understand our salvation: Jesus is the *agent* and Christianity is the *result*.

Insiders who come from Muslim backgrounds, whether they like it or not, whether they realize it or not, whether they are being discipled or not, are Christians if Jesus has saved them. It may be true that the term *Christian* carries baggage, but so what? The term *follower of Jesus* carries baggage (For instance, what is a follower? And which Jesus are you following?). The term *Messianic Muslim* favored by IMers also carries baggage (How can you compare Islam with Judaism? And what does *messiah* mean in Islam?).

I affirm that Christianity does not save us. This is the prerogative of Jesus. But what I want to hear the advocates of IM say is that insiders who are saved by Jesus are now Christian. This would parallel today's situation.

The Second

It is here the parallel ends. The first century situation is not fully parallel to the Muslims coming to faith because the gentiles were not remaining in something that is remotely related to a *socio-religious* environment. In fact the notion of a socio-religious category describing gentiles—and for the sake of the parallel argument, this must be true—is a modern day construct forced onto the text. That concept did not exist in the first century. My problem is not with the term itself, but that does not apply it to the identifier of *gentile*, thus the parallel does not exist as Lewis sees it.

Being a gentile did not mean being a member of any particular religion. It was a Jewish designation for the *non-Jew*. Non-Jews were not the children of Abraham spiritually or physically. The Jews were *ha-'am* or the people, and everyone else was *goyim* (the nations). The gentiles might worship Zeus, Athena, Apollo, Elvis (not really), all of them or none of them, but the term gentile did not refer to any one particular type of pagan. If gentile has any religious significance at all it is only in the negative; that is, a gentile is *not* a Jew.

The biblical Greek term for the non-Jews is of course, *ethne* (plural of *ethnos*), the nations. There are three synonyms for *ethnos*: *phule*, a tribe or group with common ancestry (e.g., the Hatfields and the McCoys), *laos* or people (closer to our geo-political category, such as Brazilians or Koreans), and *glossa* or tongue (e.g., Arabs). The nearest that *ethnos* comes to resembling anything religious is when the nations come to faith in Jesus (Matt 12:21, "and in his names the gentiles shall trust;" cf. Matt 21:43, 28:18-20; Mark 11:17; Luke 2:32, 24:47). Otherwise neither *ethne* nor its synonyms carry any explicit designation of religion or specific religious activity.[6]

On the other hand, the name *Muslim* does refer to something in particular. The word Muslim carries a particularistic meaning of *one who is submitted to Allah* and yet can be a very broad word that means *one who has an Islamic worldview but does not practice the faith as prescribed*. How is this parallel to the concept of gentile?

The nations were not remaining religiously the same: they left their paganism as they became Christians. Muslims are remaining as they are: they remain Muslims. This connection is not made, thus there is no parallel at this point.[7]

---

6. There is an exception to my "rule" in Matthew 6:32 when Jesus tells his disciples not to pray as the *ethne* pray. But this is not really an exception in that the word *ethne* still does not carry a socio-religious flavor to it since there is no one way the *ethne* pray, unlike Muslims who perform *salat* in essentially the same manner.

7. For a word study of *ethnos* with a missiological emphasis, see Weerstra, "Mission," 99–101. Weerstra writes, "The singular and pervasive meaning of *ethnos/ethne* throughout the Greek Scriptures is that of a people or people group, each of which is bound together by common customs, lineage, language and even the land the peoples occupy" (101).

The Third

The first century situation is not parallel to the Muslims coming to faith because the gentiles were asked to give up something—not in order to be saved, but in order to fellowship with the Jewish Christians (v. 20). They were asked to give up foods associated with the idols and sexual immorality. The idols were part of their previous lifestyle. The sexual immorality was also part and parcel of idol worship, but having become Christians these behaviors changed. There was also the turning from and turn to aspect of their conversions that does not seem to be part of the IM. But again, more on conversion in chapter 11.

On the other hand, Muslims are not giving up their previous religion, but remaining in it. The pillars of the Islamic faith may be incorporated into the living expression of the new believer's faith. This connection is not made, thus there is no parallel at this point (see Table 3, a summary of the supposed parallels).

Table 3. The lack of parallels between gentiles and Muslims.

Gentiles of Acts 15	Muslims today
Gentiles are saved without *Judaism*	Muslims are saved without *Christianity*
Gentiles *do not remain* in their previous religion	Muslims *remain* in previous religion
Gentiles *turn* from certain practices associated with idols	Muslims *do not turn* from Islam

THE INVESTIGATION'S FINDINGS: THE IMPORTANCE OF OUR VIEW OF SCRIPTURE

So far we've seen that the scriptures do not support what missionaries report is taking place among Muslims today. I think the main reason for the deficiency in sound biblical understanding may come from a wrong view of the Bible.

Our book is not a proof text, but a collection of poetry, letters, genealogies, proverbs, songs, apocalyptic, and historical narratives—the latter make up the overwhelming majority of the Old and New Testament—all bound by the one grand, sweeping theme of God's dealings with his people through history. Each genre is necessary to God's self-revelation in that every style and form provides its own unique perspective on what God has done.

As a side note, but perhaps not too far off topic, I find it interesting that the generally recognized view of inspiration[8] is parallel to our understanding that Jesus is the divinely incarnated one. As the Bible is a collection of divine books in which the author's humanity was kept in tension with the divine—human personality remains intact but submitted to the act of inspiration—so the second person of the Trinity was incarnated having both natures fully present. In other words, as Jesus was fully human and divine without a diminishing or mingling of either nature, so the Bible is fully human and fully divine. It is this view that shapes the way we interpret the Bible.

But additionally, and here I think it applies to the insider movements, what seems most notable to the incarnation is *not* that Jesus is to be incarnated into every culture of every human era. Rather the incarnation is notable for it's uniquely historical aspect. God became man. Jesus took on flesh, Jewish flesh at that. It happened in a unique way and at a distinct time. But this incarnation—again similar to the scriptural notion of *inlibration* or the Word-in-book—is not to be duplicated in every culture; rather it is transformative in culture. The transformation and uniqueness of the Word-in-flesh and the Word-in-book are first and foremost just that—unique. The singularity of those events cannot be reproduced, and therefore our understanding and interpretation of them must take this into consideration.

Now when I say the Bible is not a proof text I am really speaking about an attitude. Have you ever come up with a pretty good idea and wanted to share it with a congregation, Bible study or maybe even your dog? It's such a great idea you begin searching the scriptures for passages, any passage, that will provide even the faintest support. And lo and behold you find it! For instance, I can even prove the Bible should be my proof text: "Therefore openly before the churches, show them the proof of your love and of our reason for boasting about you" (2 Cor 8:24). An open Bible is the proof of my love.

By chucking common sense, by neglecting context (both the immediate and the larger), by trashing the normal means of interpretation and everything you learned in seminary (if you're a pastor), you craft your

---

8. See Geisler and Nix, *Introduction*, 39. They write, "Inspiration is that mysterious process by which the divine causality worked through the human prophets without destroying their individual personalities and styles to produce divinely authoritative and inerrant writings."

sermon, message, or Bible study based upon a wonderful idea that just happens to have a few Bible verses—or maybe just one—that seem to back it up.

INTERPRETATION WITH *CHUTZPAH*

It takes real chutzpah to use the Bible as a proof text. It is the height of eisegesis to approach the Bible as a collection of inspired thoughts given to support anyone's ideas. It's the pinnacle of chutzpah-ness to think we are discovering something that has been hidden for two millennia.

Is this what the advocates of IM have done? What I have just described is a very cultic use of scripture and I don't think of the proponents of the insider movements in this way. I have simply gone to the exaggerated description to point out that when we view the Bible as a book in which we believe we've discovered something new, something that has remained uncovered and mysterious awaiting the day of discovery by one with the key to scriptures, or because there is a burning in our bosom, or maybe due to the influence of "God's organization" such as the Watchtower, we are probably not interpreting God's words correctly.

So if the advocates of IM are not in the overly exaggerated position I have just described, where are they? This statement by Kevin Higgins provides us that starting point: "I see Insider Movements as fueling (and being fueled by) a rediscovery of the Incarnation, of a thoroughly biblical approach to culture and religion, of the role of the Holy Spirit in leading God's people to 'work out' the gospel in new ways, and of an understanding of how God works in the world within and beyond His covenant people."[9]

I sense an underlying brazenness in this statement. There is a *rediscovery*, a new *working out* of the gospel, and all of it *beyond* God's covenant with his people—sure he also says within the covenant, but this is not where we disagree. The notion that God would work beyond or outside of his own covenant is an idea than fell out of the ugly tree and hit every branch on the way down. This is very disturbing at a visceral level. There seems to exist a view of the scriptures in which something that was hidden has finally been unearthed. The archeologist's spade has broken through the final layer of dirt to reveal a previously unknown treasure. It's like someone gave a Bible to Indiana Jones.

9. Higgins, "The Key," 155–56.

We are touching on theology of religions with Higgins' comment that God is moving "beyond His covenant people." Is it too off base to think we are being introduced to a third covenant; that is, a covenant beyond the last covenant? Has God given the Old Covenant of the law of Moses, followed by the New Covenant (introduced within the context of the Old Covenant) fulfilled in the Messiah, but he has waited until *now* to reveal a third covenant? Is this the direction of the IM? What prevents us from discovering God moving beyond the *beyond-his-covenant-people* into a fourth covenant? I know I'm exaggerating, but it's to drive a point home.

BACK TO WHERE WE BEGAN

Let's bring all of this back to Acts 15. Remember the emphasis upon the observations and reports from the field missionaries to the council? The observations of the advocates of insider movements are the spade of discovery. These observations actually help us interpret the scriptures; that is, the missionary's studied surveillance brings light to God's word. That troubles me, too.

I know, I know; the advocates of IM disagree with my assessment. They do not believe that what I'm describing accurately portrays what they believe about scripture and how they interpret it. I will grant that, but I *am* saying this is what I see happening. It seems a logical implication from what at least one of them has written.

I want to reemphasize what I believe to be a proper view of scripture and its message: the gospel is first and foremost transformational in its operation. The scripture is a record of what God has done, a guarantee that what we trust in and rely on—the death, burial, resurrection and soon coming of Jesus—is real. Scripture is not first and foremost (nor even third and fourth-most) a model for what God is doing in the twenty-first century among the Hindus, Buddhists, and Muslims. Scripture is the message of a new life in Christ.

The hunt for a parallel universe, that tangible connection between Acts 15 and Muslim ministry today, has not proven to be a boon, but a black hole. Such an interpretation sucks into it the better understanding of the teachings of Acts 15. So let's all take a deep breath and thank God for his preservation of his Word. And let's all take a step back from our preconceived notions of what the Word *implies* into our situations and rather ask, what does the Word teach.

8

Acts 17, By Jupiter, I Think He's Got It!

PAUL'S SERMON ON MARS Hill is one of the most widely discussed episodes in missions. What does the passage teach us? How much and how far can we contextualize to our audience as we share the good news? Or is there a different lesson to learn, maybe?

ACTS 17:22–23, 28

22 So Paul stood in the midst of the Areopagus and said, "Men of Athens, I observe that you are very religious in all respects. 23 For while I was passing through and examining the objects of your worship, I also found an altar with this inscription, 'TO AN UNKNOWN GOD.' Therefore what you worship in ignorance, this I proclaim to you. . . . 28 for in Him we live and move and exist, as even some of your own poets have said, 'For we also are His children.'"

THE ISSUES

In the case of Paul in Athens, it seems there are least three issues worthy of mentioning: (1) the question of identity; (2) discovering if God is at work in pagan religions (i.e., theology of religions); (3) and if the missionary may use the texts of Islam as a bridge. Rebecca Lewis speaks about identity, followed by Higgins on theology of religions, and then on the use of Islam's scriptures:

> 1. In the case of insider movements alone, this new spiritual identity is not combined with a change of socio-political-religious

identity. The scriptures seem to indicate that this identity, and the community a person is born into, were determined in advance by God. For example, Paul declares to the Athenians that God "made every nation of men . . . and determined the times set for them and the exact places they should live" (Acts 17:26). When we encourage believers to remain in their families and networks, and to retain their birth identities, we honor these God-given relationships.[1]

2. There is a sense in which he [Paul] sees the altar to the unknown god as preparation for what he will say about the gospel. . . . we need to remind ourselves of what is really taking place. A Jewish monotheist (Paul) is using a pagan altar as a sign that the people he addresses are religious and that they have in fact been worshipping the true God without knowing it. This is not the same thing as saying that this "anonymous worship" is salvific. I am not arguing that, nor do I believe it. But Paul is assuming they have been worshipping the true God without knowing Him.[2]

3. An insider approach can freely use religious and secular aspects of the culture to communicate biblical truth. This includes the texts and ceremonies of the religion one is seeking to reach. Missionaries should not fear that doing so might cause others to confuse them as being "Muslim" or "Hindu."[3]

IN OTHER WORDS

(1) According to Acts 17:26, Lewis believes scripture wants us to value birth, culture, and socio-politico-religious identities. (2) Kevin Higgins sees in Acts 17 the implication that God has placed certain signs or phenomena in religions that help non-Jews come to faith in Yahweh. (3) Finally, Higgins also believes Acts 17 is the sanction for using the Qur'an in evangelization.

1. YOU AREN'T WHO YOU THINK YOU ARE

Identity is one of the key issues of the insider movements.[4] Proponents of IM speak of one's religious identity, socio-religious identity, cultural

1. Lewis, "Insider Movements," 17.
2. Higgins, "The Key," 161.
3. Ibid., 162.
4. Cf. Rick Brown, "Biblical Muslims." *IJFM* 2:2 (2007): 65–74; Rick Brown, "Muslims

identity, Muslim identity, Islamic communal identity, and so forth. None of IM's critics, myself included, minimize the notion of identity, but I do marvel at the extraordinary emphasis upon every identity except our identity with the Body of Christ. Acts 17:26 is cited as evidence the Bible honors "God-given relationships," which really means whatever community one has the (mis)fortune to be born in is God-given: i.e., Hindu, Buddhist, Muslim, Satanic, agnostic, Baalistic, prostitutionistic, Baptist, or cannibalistic. Is that possible?

Let's do some quick exegesis of verses 26–27, as we will want to focus on the meaning of "appointed times and the boundaries of their habitation." These verses are part of Paul's gospel appeal to the Athenians. His preaching presents these themes: first, the recognition of the Athenian polytheism, yet ignorance of God (vv.22–23); second, God as creator, not the created ("does not dwell in temples," vv.24–25); and third, Paul directly confronts the Athenian worldview. It is this last point I want to address.

The Athenians believed they sprang up from the very soil of Athens[5] (giving rise to the philosopher Bromikos' somewhat soiled proverb, "Bloom where you're planted"). Paul's statement that God made all humans from one man goes against what the Athenians thought of themselves. It seems quite likely Paul is referring to Adam as that one man.[6] This makes sense as he is speaking of the God of creation.

Next there are two infinitive phrases we need to consider: "*to live* on all the face of the earth and *to seek* God." This is man's purpose: to live and to seek God. It also fits with the Genesis account that man is created in the image of God. So without ever mentioning scripture, Paul is preaching a biblical message to the Athenians.

Inserted between these two infinitives of purpose are the terms I want to think about: "appointed times and the boundaries of their habitation." Lewis takes *appointed times* and *boundaries* to refer to identity. I would agree in part, but I believe she missed the real thrust of the passage.

Who Believe the Bible." *MF* (July-August 2008): 19–23; Frank Decker, "When 'Christian' Does Not Translate." *MF* (September-October 2005): 8; Harley Talman, "Comprehensive Contextualization." *IJFM* 21:1 (2004): 6–12; H. L. Richard, "Unpacking the Insider Paradigm: An Open Discussion on Points of Diversity." *IJFM* 26:4 (2009): 175–80; J. Dudley Woodberry, "To the Muslim I Became a Muslim?" *IJFM* 24:1 (2007): 23–28.

5. Bruce, *Acts*, 337.
6. Cf. Witherington, *Acts*, 526.

Acts 14:17 has a similar phrase translated as *seasons*. The word is qualified by "rains from heaven" so that it is easily understood as seasons of the year; however, there is no such qualification in Acts 17:26. This makes the interpretation of "appointed times" a period of history as more likely, and therefore "boundaries" as national and geographical borders. Witherington speaks to the implications of this interpretation: "This comports nicely with and probably draws upon Deut. 32:8, which reads: 'When the Most High apportioned the nations, when he divided humankind, he fixed the boundaries of the people according to the number of the gods.' . . . On the basis of the Deuteronomic text multiple gods and multiple nations go together, and by the same token if God is working to unite all peoples in Christ, crossing national boundaries, then God is also working against polytheism."[7]

Yes, Paul had identity in mind, but not as Lewis imagines it. If God is *working against* polytheism, it's hard to understand how he might be *working within* it, as Lewis suggests. What Paul seems to be saying to the parochial Athenians is this: "God made all humanity from one person. The notion of boundaries and many gods, and eras, the rise and fall of kingdoms, all these point to one thing: God is bringing about the unification of all humanity under the leadership of one man, Jesus Christ." If I may put it in terms readily understood by the advocates of IM: the Messianic Muslims having an Islamic identity—something you advocates of IM encourage them to keep—is not as important as the identity God has created for them in Jesus. In fact, there is no socio-religious, community identity, or cultural identity that unites like Jesus.

The notion of a God-given identity is 180 degrees different as a close look at the passage shows. The suggestion of a multicultural identity that emphasizes one's minority identity at the neglect of the majority does not fit.

Let me draw an analogy from the political life of the United States. We are a nation of immigrants. We like other cultures; we enjoy Little Saigon, Little Tokyo, Little Gaza, and Chinatown. But as a body of immigrants, we are often beguiled by a plurality of identities: "I'm a Maldivian-Xhosan-Caribbean-American, and that's just on my mother's side." I think we have forgotten that *e pluribus unum*, from the many come one, is who

---

7. Ibid., 527.

we are as Americans. When it comes to our allegiance to our country, we are Americans. Period.

Analogously Christ is the great unifier and identity-giver. He makes one body from the many cultural identities—*e pluribus unum est ecclesia*, that is, the church is one from the many. Let me hasten to add that when we do become one with Christ in the Body at our conversion, we are not giving up our cultural identity. Our union and identification with the Trinitarian God simply overshadows, outweighs, and minimizes our cultural identity. Our identity with Jesus exceeds the human desire for cultural identity, or our "seasons and boundaries."

2. PAGAN ALTARS

Did Paul see something significant in the pagan religion of the Athenians? Was there "a sign that the people he addresses are religious and that they have in fact been worshipping the true God without knowing it"? Is Higgins right? As I did with the claim above, a brief examination of the passage is necessary (17:22–23 specifically).

Religious or Superstitious?

What should we think about Paul's recognition of the Athenians' religiosity (v. 22, the Greek is *deisidaimonesterous*)? Most of us probably understand this as if Paul had addressed a gathering of Bible Belt Americans saying, "Men and women of Athens, Georgia, I observe that you are very spiritual (*deisidaimonesterous*) in every way." I don't believe Paul meant it this way at all. A speaker at the Areopagus was not to flatter the audience in his introductory remarks with the intent of buttering them up to accept his premise.[8] Additionally, when you examine Paul's approach in other cities, he never flatters his audience, but confronts them, speaking plainly (see Acts 13:9–11, 16–41, 46–47, 51; 14:1, 7, 14–18, 21–22). So it makes better sense to interpret Paul's comment about their religiosity as *superstition*. "I see you are quite superstitious," he told the Athenians. A better parallel would have Paul speaking at the local Baptist church, saying, "I understand you Baptists are very religious (*deisidaimonesterous*), but do you know Jesus?" It's not meant as a compliment. And if this is correct, it seems unlikely Paul is hopeful the pagan altars are stepping-stones to faith. They are more like impediments.

8. Bruce, *Acts*, 335.

Preparation for the Gospel?

Is the pagan altar used by God to prepare the Athenians for the gospel? This is open for disagreement because if we consider the results of his preaching, one could say most of the Athenians were not prepared for the message. They rejected it. Though to be fair, the argument of preparation followed by rejection can also apply to the rejection of Messiah by the very people *most* prepared for him. Of course a major difference between the preparations afforded the Jews and that allegedly provided to the Athenians is that the former was special revelation while the latter was not.

So without too much ado, I simply disagree with this idea, although I cannot point to anything in the passage that would support my view any more than it might negate it.

The Role of Natural Revelation

What about the claim the Athenians had been worshipping the one true God without even knowing it? Paul did say, "What therefore you worship in ignorance, this I proclaim to you." It seems possible there was some level of ignorance and worship simultaneously, but whether the Athenians' ignorance outweighed their sincerity of worship is unknown; that is, they really did not know what they were doing. If that is the case, it seems to me that such an act of worship is futility multiplied by lack of awareness.

Paul's statement of their ignorance sounds a lot like his Romans chapter 1 treatise on natural revelation. There he speaks of how nature reveals the handiwork of God, offering hints to the open-minded that he is present. Is this what took place among the Athenians? Of course, as Higgins says, there was nothing salvific about the Athenian's ignorance or their worship; we are agreed on this. The major point at which we disagree is that Higgins believes these altars are the work of God deliberately placed by him into other religions with the *intent* they act as signs. Where we differ is at the point of God's intention.

I know God intended that we see him in creation: "For since the creation of the world His invisible attributes, His eternal power and divine nature, have been clearly seen, being understood through what has been made, so that they are without excuse" (Rom 1:20). God's intention is explicitly stated in the scriptures. Creation points to the existence of a maker, a designer, and a creator. I hesitate calling anything in a nature an altar, but if the ocean's grandeur, a sunset's deep red-orange glow, or the wind moving mightily though the redwoods is a demonstration of the creator's presence, then perhaps these are altars or signs. But, I do not know that God intended to reflexively point to himself from inside other religions. This conclusion can only be reached because it is brought to the passage; it does not clearly reside in the text at all. The conclusion appears to push the passage beyond it's intended meaning.

Additionally, that Yahweh would deliberately place pointers to his presence in other religions presents us with some problematic issues. First, an altar/sign is easily misconstrued. I may look at Hinduism and see the existence of the ten avatars with number ten still to come. The descriptions of the tenth and coming avatar, *Kalki*, seem Christlike to the Christian. The *Kalki Purana* describes him coming at an auspicious time in history, on a white horse, carrying a sword, and delivering the world from evil. But it is only the Christian who would make the connection that Kalki resembles Jesus. Worshippers of *Kalkideva* would not conclude this for they know *Kalki* is an incarnation of *Vishnu*, not Jesus. Is this an altar/sign in Hinduism? It's easy for the non-Hindu to believe it is. The Hindu simply shrugs his shoulders when told the comparison by missionaries. The incarnation of Vishnu is far different than the incarnation of the Word of God.

Second, and the more problematic reason for concluding Yahweh has painted road signs to himself in other religions is that by doing so, Yahweh lends authenticity, however slight it might be, to the credibility of that religion. This contradicts the nature of our God as he has revealed himself. He is jealous for his people that they not serve other gods (Deut 4:23–25). Why should we think Yahweh would condone any part of another religious tradition that is, as Higgins himself has said, "the rejection of the truth of God"?

So with regard to the pagan altars hinting at, pointing to, or preparing pagans for God, I do not even understand these altars as natural revelation. If God has made himself known without equivocation in the natural world, as Paul said, why would he do so within religions that do not bring him honor and are by their nature demonic?[9]

---

9. For an interesting treatment on a theology of religions, see McDermott, *Can Evangelicals Learn from World Religions?* 92: "There is radical discontinuity between the religions and the Christ: Christ is a Being before whom all other beings and manifestations of God are separated by an infinite qualitative difference. There may exist

3. POET NOT PROPHET AND POEM NOT SCRIPTURE

Paul cites the Cretan, Epimenides (v. 28), and Aratus the Cilician. Epimenides wrote a poem in honor of Zeus, which Paul contextualized to speak about Yahweh. From Aratus he took the fifth line from his *Phaenomena*, a poem dedicated to Jupiter.[10] Paul calls both of the men poets, not prophets. He says their works are poems, not scriptures.[11] I have to completely disagree with the conclusion that this passage commends the use of other scriptures for the purposes of the gospel. Paul cited poetry, not divinely authoritative texts.

Furthermore Higgins encourages missionaries to use the "ceremonies of the religion one is seeking to reach." I am unaware of how the passage in Acts 17 can be used to make this argument—and nowhere is the claim substantiated by any of the proponents of IM (except perhaps by Woodberry, chapter 10). Where are there ceremonies of the Athenians listed or described for us; and where is there an example of any religious activity taking place in the chapter? Without Higgins' actually showing us from the text of Acts 17 how he arrived at his implications, they remain unfounded opinions.

JUPITER HAS NOTHING TO DO WITH IT!

IM understands Acts 17:26 as proving there is value in cultural and sociopolitical identity, that other religions have altars or signs that point to the existence of Yahweh, and that since Paul used other scriptures, so may we. I believe I've made it clear that each of these conclusions strains the text.

In the case of our identity, Paul's comments are really a confrontation of the Athenian worldview. He does not affirm our ethnic, linguistic,

---

revelations *from* God in other religions, but only in the religion of the Christ is there the revelation *of* God as incarnate in Jesus of Nazareth." McDermott does not so much agree with either Higgins or me (though I think more with Kevin than me), but he offers a third position. He suggests that God can use various elements of other religious traditions to bring about repentance or to bring them into knowledge of Jesus, although the non-biblical religion must not be seen as a stepping-stone or structurally linked to the full knowledge of Jesus. McDermott does not speak of Yahweh actually working in another religion or being in relationship with pagans, neither does he discount the value of certain truths that tap into biblical truths.

10. Calvin in Bruce, *Acts,* 339.

11. Neither Bruce, Fernando, Tannehill, nor Witherington call these authors anything but poets or philosophers and their writings poems. I am unaware of any scholar who makes the case for these poems to be scriptures.

religious identities as God-given, rather he calls us to recognize the oneness we share in Jesus, the Lord of the church.

I conceded the ambiguity of altars or signs in other religions, but encourage you to remember the passage is silent on the matter. Whereas Paul is explicit about natural revelation as a pointer to the existence of God, the notion of altars is not explicit to the text, but relies on the reader bringing the idea to the text.

Finally, on the matter of Paul's use of scriptures from other religions, this conclusion is without merit. Paul did not use scriptures, but poetry. He did not cite prophets, but poets.

And Olympus, recognizing its irrelevancy, wept.

9

First Corinthians 7, Christian Remains

No, this is not a chapter on how we should bury our dead. Here I want to think about the nature of Islam with regard to the new believer. If Islam is a socio-religious system, and the religion of Islam is just a part of that all-encompassing system, it makes sense for converts to Jesus from Muslim backgrounds to stay connected with their cultural heritage. Right?

FIRST CORINTHIANS 7:17–20

17 Only, as the Lord has assigned to each one, as God has called each, in this manner let him walk. And so I direct in all the churches. 18 Was any man called when he was already circumcised? He is not to become uncircumcised. Has anyone been called in uncircumcision? He is not to be circumcised. 19 Circumcision is nothing, and uncircumcision is nothing, but what matters is the keeping of the commandments of God. 20 Each man must remain in that condition in which he was called.

THE ISSUE

Commenting on v. 20, Rebecca Lewis writes:

> At first it appears that Paul was saying that the Lord has assigned to each of us the family and people group we are born into, and when He calls us to Himself, He also calls us to reach out to those around us in that community and not remove ourselves from that situation. However, the crux of Paul's argument is actually that no one should consider one religious form of faith in Christ to be

superior to another. "What counts," Paul emphasized, is " faith expressing itself in love," "keeping God's commands," and becoming "a new creation." As believers we need to be able to look past differences in religious culture and see the Holy Spirit working in the lives of our fellow citizens of the Kingdom.[1]

IN OTHER WORDS

Paul is encouraging Jews who come to Christ to remain Jews and gentiles should remain gentiles. The implication is that Muslims may remain Muslims.

DIGGING UP THE "REMAINS"

Paul tells each Corinthian to "remain in that condition in which he was called." So, if you are Muslim, be a Muslim who follows Jesus. My first take on this interpretation is that it sets off my *bad-vibes-o-meter*. It just doesn't feel right, but I can't quite say why. So, let's root around in the hole that has been dug for us and see what remains we can find.

Who Are You?

The issue here is identity—or is it? Let the Jews be Jews; let the gentiles be gentiles. Lewis writes, "Paul emphasized the importance of the gospel *not* being linked to changing cultures, even religious cultures."[2] This is something we can all agree to. Those who come to Christ do not do so by initially becoming Swiss, Egyptians, or Nigerians. Paul is indeed speaking to the gentiles and reminding them they do not have to become Jews in order to be Christians. The problem is that Lewis is making an application that is ill-founded; that is, let the Muslim remain a Muslim.

Context

Chapter 7 focuses on several questions Paul is attempting to answer. First he deals with entering marriage relations (vv. 1-9). Barnes suggests the problem may have come up because of an argument between the gentile and Jewish believers.[3] The gentiles, perhaps influenced by Greek philoso-

---

1. Lewis, "Integrity," 46.
2. Ibid.
3. Barnes, *1 Corinthians*.

phy that pretty much advised against marriage, struggled to see its value, versus the Jewish believers who understood marriage as a sacrament. Paul's answer to the possible tension between the Greeks and Jews is that if you are not married, don't get married; but if you are married, stay married. Remain in the condition you were in when God called you to himself. The second question (vv. 10–24) springs out of the first: should a married believer stay married to a spouse who is not also a believer? The general principle seems to be that the believer should stay married.

Here is how the passage lays out:

v.10, Wives, don't leave your unconverted husbands.

v.11, Escape clause: what to do if the spouse leaves.

v.12, Christian men stay married to unbelieving wives.

v.13, Christian women stay married to unbelieving husbands.

v.14, The benefit of marriage.

v.15, If the unbelieving spouse wants to leave, allow him or her to leave.

v.16, A question for the believing spouse.

v.17, Believers must live in their God-given assignments.

v.18–19, This is a possible parenthetical statement for the sake of illustration: circumcision and uncircumcision do not matter; what matters is obedience (such as not divorcing one's spouse just because he or she is not a Christian).

The point of Paul's comments is that Christianity is not a religion in which every believer is somehow made discontent with his lot in life. Following Jesus does not make the believer unhappy with his condition or environment; rather believing Jesus is Lord offers a meaning to one's life that surpasses one's situation.

Remain in Your Klésis

So we come to verse 20 in which Paul writes about our *klésis* (condition or vocation). This does not refer to some type of socio-religious context or religious community. A simple word study shows that Paul had *calling* or *vocation* in mind by its use (Alford, Barnes, Biblical Illustrator, Calvin, et al.) The list of commentators who take the word klésis to mean one's condition or vocation in life is overwhelming. I am unaware of any reputable commentary that makes the case for klésis as socio-religious environment—though I could be corrected.

From verse 20 forward, Paul speaks about slavery. There is nothing religious about slavery and he ends his comments in verse 24 with the refrain "each one is to remain with God in that condition (implied) in which he is called." Paul then picks up the marriage theme again (vv. 25–40). There is nothing in the passage that speaks of a socio-religious environment or religious community in which the believer is to remain.

Real Identity

But suppose we give the interpretation I believe to be misguided the benefit of some considerable doubt, that is, *condition* refers to one's socio-religious environment and identity. Any verse that emphasizes Jewish and gentile identity ought to be held to the standard of Galatians 3:26–28. Paul reminds the churches of Galatia that the identifiers of Jews and Greeks (gentiles), slave and free, male and female are forever changed by new birth in Christ. "For you are all one in Christ Jesus. And if you belong to Christ, then you are Abraham's descendants, heirs according to promise." There is some leeway to how we might understand this change, but the fact is clear: our identity is in Christ, not in our ethnicity (in the case of the gentiles) or our religion and our culture (Jews). David Horrell writes a concise summary of the situation: "Paul's corporate Christology provides the basis for his conviction that all who are in Christ have died to the old era and now live (corporately) as 'one,' a new creation, the body of Christ, in the power of the Spirit: *former distinctions signify nothing*" (emphasis mine)[4]

I believe it can be rightly said that our ethnicity and cultural identification are eternally altered upon our confession of Christ. As we grow in Christ, we realize how eternally unimportant our own culture is—and how evil it is in so many ways. Knowing Jesus brings us into a larger community, the kingdom of God, that is best described not as ethnically free, but ethnically minimized. Our ethnicity and cultures are not eradicated by new birth in Jesus, they are just put in their proper perspective.

I believe God enjoys cultures; he made us and culture is part of our expression. But we are also sinners, and as such, sin infects our culture, values, beliefs, and worldviews.

---

4. Horrell, "No Longer Jew or Greek," 25.

ISLAM: CULTURE OR RELIGION?

One assumption about theology of religions held by the proponents of IM has to do with the nature of Islam. Is Islam a culture or a religion? Let me speak briefly about culture especially as it relates to Islam. We need to try to tease apart the idea of culture and religion, which seems easy at first glance, but with Islam it is tricky. In some ways it is both a culture and religion, although virtually any Muslim you meet with tell you Islam is just a way of life, a complete way of living. That means it is religion, culture, social grouping, etc. So, I think we can all agree Islam is a religion, but how is Islam a culture?

Most of us who have studied Islam agree that the religion has cultural elements knit into it. Islam does provide every Muslim a new culture regardless his or her own secular culture. This Islamic culture is called the *sunna* of the prophet that is recorded in the *hadith*.

Sunna means *way of acting*. It has come to mean the way the prophet of Islam behaved. The hadith, meaning *report*, contains his behaviors, his disapprovals of various actions, and even the actions of some of the earliest Muslims. These traditions are the manner in which Muslims live their lives today nearly 1400 years after the death of their prophet.

Muslims perform *salat*, the five-times-a-day prayer; this is sunna. I have attended many prayer times in the mosque and noticed how often a father will correct his son or daughter when they make a mistake during salat. Maybe their hand is in the wrong place or they bowed too soon. The father gently corrects the child because the form of salat must be done correctly. If it is not, the prayer is invalid.

Where does this understanding come from that salat must be done exactly the same way by all Muslims everywhere? It comes from the life of Muhammad. Muhammad received the form of salat from Allah's emissary, the angel Gabriel. The main implication for Muslims is this: do not tamper with the form because the form is the meaning; the meaning and function is found in the form. To bow, bend the knees, to touch one's forehead to the ground, and all the rest of the prayer form signifies *prayer and worship*.

The implication for the believer who comes out of Islam is that to remain in Islam, to continue to perform salat, no matter that he or she is praying to Yahweh, the convert is, in fact, performing a ritual that proclaims a Muslim identity as one who is submitted to the Allah of the Qur'an.

Muslims perform the obligatory prayers because Muhammad said so. Salat has a divinely revealed form and meaning. How can this form be filled with Christian meaning when Islam itself determines the meaning? Should a Muslim see a Christian performing salat he will think that person is a Muslim—not a Christian giving new meaning to salat.

The implication for the missionary is to stop encouraging new believers to "*remain* in" Islam. Help them discover the freedom of worship they have in Christ, the one who gives them their identity.

TINKER OR PILGRIM?

There are two prevailing views of culture among most missionaries. Chuck Kraft propounds the first and perhaps predominant view. He believes culture is neutral, acting as path upon which we walk. The path does not necessarily constrain a person to walk on it; one can certainly leave it at any time, but generally we stay on the path because it is provides us security and identity. We know where we're going.

Sherwood Lingenfelter suggests an opposing, and more appropriate view (in my opinion) of culture, especially for work among Muslims. According to Lingenfelter, culture is not neutral; rather culture is a prison from which we need to escape. Since man is sinful, he creates sinful structures; these sinful structures are our cultures. There is not much neutrality in culture if it is sinful. It is therefore the goal of discipleship to lead a person out of the bondage of culture into the freedom of knowing Christ. Every follower of Jesus, every Christian, is on a pilgrimage away from his culture, his prison of bondage, and into full obedience to Jesus. Do not think that this means the believer stops being a Kurd, a Uighur, or a Navaho. Rather it is an awareness that as a Christian the culture of one's birth is not one's prime identifier. In fact, following Jesus brings an awareness of the evils of the birth culture. So part of the pilgrimage may be to actually redeem sinful cultural values and beliefs, making them more biblical where possible.

I hope you can see the implications of either view. If you believe Kraft is right, it becomes natural to decontextualize the forms of Islam, thinking we can baptize them with new meaning. After all, there is nothing inherently wrong with shahada, salat, zakat, sawm, or hajj the proponents of IM would argue. With caution and the guidance of the Spirit, these forms may be adapted to a Christian setting. So, the Christian becomes a tinker, a fixer-upper, and an experimenter.

On the other hand, if Lingenfelter is right, upon confession of Christ, the convert begins the discipleship process of an increasing awareness of the sinfulness, not only himself, but his culture as well. Discipleship from this perspective will look like a pilgrimage. The Christian is a pilgrim and previous religious forms are seen as unacceptable and unbiblical.[5]

PUTTING THE "REMAINS" TO REST

Could Paul possibly be encouraging Muslims to remain Muslim? Would he tell a Mormon to remain a Mormon or a homosexual to remain in the homosexual culture? Paul says, "Remain in that condition," but does he mean to be a Mormon Background Believer or a Homosexual Background Believer?

Let me be clear. The 1 Corinthians 7 passage is directed toward gentiles and Jews. Gentiles were not to become Jewish proselytes. We all agree to this. The rub comes when we press Islam into the text. Islam is not Judaism; neither is Islam gentile-ism (if there is such a word). Attempting to push Islam into the passage may seem like a simple attempt to make an application, but this moves beyond application. Plopping Islam into the passage changes the intent of what Paul is teaching: i.e., our larger unity in Christ despite our cultural differences.

---

5. To read more about this subject, see: Charles Kraft, *Anthropology for Christian Witness*. Orbis, 1996; Sherwood Lingenfelter, *Transforming Culture*. Baker, 1998.

10

First Corinthians 9, To the Mormon I became as a Mormon

Are Christians chameleons, changing color to match the environment? Is the Christian strategy to become like our audience in order to trick them into a hearing for the gospel?

FIRST CORINTHIANS 9:19-23

19 For though I am free from all *men*, I have made myself a slave to all, so that I may win more. 20 To the Jews I became as a Jew, so that I might win Jews; to those who are under the Law, as under the Law though not being myself under the Law, so that I might win those who are under the Law; 21 to those who are without law, as without law, though not being without the law of God but under the law of Christ, so that I might win those who are without law. 22 To the weak I became weak, that I might win the weak; I have become all things to all men, so that I may by all means save some. 23 I do all things for the sake of the gospel, so that I may become a fellow partaker of it.

THE ISSUE

J. Dudley Woodberry has written most extensively on this topic. Here he develops the case for missionaries becoming a Muslim to the Muslim:

> God sent his Son to be incarnated under the same Law that guided the people whom he sought to redeem . . . Therefore, as we follow Jesus we might go under a similar Law—or remain under that

Law—for the redemption of those under that Law. . . . First, Jesus observed the Mosaic Law, but rejected any traditions of the elders that conflicted with the teachings of scripture. And he internalized and deepened its meaning in the Sermon on the Mount. . . . Second, Qur'anic and Islamic Law in general draw heavily on Jewish Law with its roots in Mosaic Law . . . The Qur'an even includes all of the Ten Commandments . . . Therefore, although there are some differences, much of Islamic Law is similar to Mosaic Law and can be internalized and interpreted as fulfilled in Christ. Thirdly, the leaders of the Temple and synagogues had corrupted Judaic worship and rejected Jesus, but he and his first followers continued to identify with Judaism and to participate in temple and synagogue worship. Therefore a case can be made for Muslims who follow Jesus to continue to identify with their Muslim community and participate, to the extent their consciences allow, in its religious observance.[1]

IN OTHER WORDS

The conclusion Woodberry suggests has less to do with Jesus and an exegesis of 1 Corinthians 9 than it does with the nature of Islam. He concludes that the similarity of Islamic law to the Mosaic law allows converts from Islam to fulfill the Mosaic by following Jesus while remaining in Islam, just as the early believers remained Jewish. Furthermore, the forms and rituals of Islam, since they originated with Judaism and Christianity, may be adapted for use by new converts from Islam.

EXEGESIS OF THE PASSAGE

Before speaking to Woodberry's observations and conclusions, we need to look at the passage. What is Paul's emphasis in the passage? Where is he going with his thoughts? How do we put these words into action? And perhaps more importantly, do Paul's statements support the IM strategy of Muslim evangelism?

The Larger Context

Chapter 9 is part of larger portion of scripture, arguably chapters 8 and 9 and much of 10 in which Paul's major theme is the liberty of the believer in Christ. The question seems to revolve around how believers should

1. Woodberry, "To the Muslim," 24.

respond to the invitation to eat meat that has been offered to idols. (8:1). Paul's principle is that the strong believer, that is, the Christian who understands that idols are nothing (8:4–6), does not cash in on this knowledge, rather expresses his willingness to forgo his liberty out of love for the weaker brother, that is one who does not understand his liberty in Christ. Notice how Paul consistently juxtaposes his liberty in Christ with what he actually does:

- 8:1–3, Knowledge (about true identity of idols) is not as important as acting in love.
- 8:4–13, Liberty to eat meat offered to idols should not cause a weak brother to stumble (liberty vs. love)
- 9:1–14, The rights of an apostle are tempered by his actions (vv. 15–18).

The Climax

In 9:19–23 Paul begins to bring to a climax his point about our relationship to others in the body of Christ. Liberty is always tempered by love. Our freedom in Christ must not become a stumbling block. Our freedom is not freedom if it enslaves believers. Using this principle, Paul begins his final statements:

- 9:19, "I have made myself a slave to all." This is Paul's liberty being redirected from what he can do that pleases himself in order to be the servant of others. Paul's freedom does not mean he is free to do as he pleases, rather to become the slave or servant to others. In other words, Paul's freedom allows him to consider the needs of others over his own rights. Paul writes, *emouton edoulōsa*, "I enslaved myself."[2] He did not take on the shackles of slavery; rather he took the attitude of a slave, a servant, one whose rights are not considered higher than the one he serves.
- 9:20–21, "To the Jews I became as a Jew." Paul did not say he became a Jew. He *did* say he became "as a Jew." He lived as a Jew among Jews. He did not announce he was no longer following Jesus to once again be a disciple of Moses, but "he carefully observed the

---

2. Robertson, *Word Pictures*, 147.

ceremonies of the law."[3] The same is true for gentiles or "those who are without law."

- 9:22–23, "To the weak I became weak…I do all things for the sake of the gospel." This is the climax of the question asked in 8:1. Paul's liberty is Christ is a given, but this liberty does not stand in the way of appearing weak (not eating meat). His liberty does not interfere with not actualizing his rights as an apostle. His liberty does not hinder him from being as a Jew or as one without the law. Paul's climax is that his love, his tenderness, his compassion, and his willingness to limit his liberty is how he "may by all means save some."

BACK TO WOODBERRY

I stated above that Woodberry's article has less to do with 1 Corinthians 9 than with the nature of Islam. His article really does not exegete or explain the passage. What his article does is to cite the passage, jump to the C1–C5 Spectrum, various models of incarnation (Jesus, Paul, and the Jerusalem Council), all the while assuming the reality and biblical support for insider movements. It is not until near the end of his article that he writes about 1 Corinthians 8:1–13 from which he immediately jumps into an application for today's missionaries among Muslims.

I appreciate and share Woodberry's enthusiasm to see Muslims come to Christ. I just wonder if 1 Corinthians 9:19–23 supports the insider movements strategies as it is assumed it does.

THE 8.5 COMMANDMENTS

Before I get too far into examining Woodberry's conclusions, I want to speak to one of his statements that I believe is mistaken. Woodberry writes, "The Qur'an even includes all of the Ten Commandments." I have heard this many times from Christians who are sympathetic to Islam. It is my conviction this is incorrect. I could create a chart with a word for word comparison of the Ten Commandments in the Bible compared to the Qur'an, but that is not necessary. Instead, Table 4 below lists the Ten Commandments from both books in a summary fashion.

---

3. Calvin, *Commentary*.

Table 4. A comparison of the Ten Commandments from the Bible and Qur'an.

Exodus 20	Qur'an	Same?
No other gods	No other gods (Q28:70)	Yes and NO
No idols	No idols (Q14:35)	Yes
Do not use God's name in vain	Do not use God's name in an oath as an excuse for doing good (Q2:224)	Yes?
Keep sabbath holy	Muslims pray Friday (Q62:9)	NO
Honor parents	Honor parents (Q46:15)	Yes
Do not murder	Do not murder (but debatable) (Q17:33)	Yes and NO
Do not commit adultery	Do not commit adultery (Q17:32)	Yes
Do not steal	Do not steal (Q60:12)	Yes
Do not steal	Do not lie (Q2:42)	Yes
Do not covet	Do not covet (Q15:88)	Yes

Woodberry argues that Islam's book contains the same commandments as the Bible. As you can see I don't believe this is the case. The first commandment is to have no other gods. It's true that the Qur'an has the equivalent to the biblical command, but Woodberry appears to assume that Allah is Yahweh. Of significant irony to this assumption is that Allah *may not* have led Israel out of Egypt according to the story in the Qur'an. The biblical command begins with the admonition to remember, "I am the Lord your God, who brought you out of the land of Egypt." The Qur'an never tells us Allah led the Jews out of Egypt; in fact, it implies Allah *may* have given the Jews Egypt as their promised land (Q26:52–59; 28:2–6). I admit the claim Allah did not lead the Jews out of Egypt is shady, so the assumption that Allah spoke a similar commandment as Yahweh earns a fifty percent equivalency—a "yes" and "no."[4]

4. This book is not the place for a full investigation into the identity of Allah vis-à-vis Yahweh. But a simple comparison of Allah and Yahweh shows at least five major differences that I believe conclusively show they cannot be the same. 1) Allah is not immanent, but only transcendent. He does not walk in the garden with Adam and Eve; does not speak with Abraham at the oaks of Mamre; does not wrestle with Judah, and so forth. 2) Allah is not interested in human beings in a personal manner. Qur'an 11:119 shows Allah promising to fill hell with the jinn and human beings. 3) Allah never makes a covenant 4) with his covenant people who, as part of their worship, 5) build a temple. These last three

The third commandment, "You shall not take the name of the Lord your God in vain" is wrongly equated with using God's name in an oath. The meaning of the biblical commandment is not to take God's name as the source of authority thus lending credibility to your actions. But as this interpretation is open for discussion, I will give the command's equivalence the benefit of the doubt.

The fourth commandment is to keep the sabbath holy. Within the context of the commandments given in Exodus 20 Yahweh details the sabbath day for the Jews. First he tells us to whom the sabbath belongs: "the seventh day is a sabbath of the Lord your God" (v. 10). The day is the Lord's, not man's. Mankind is not the owner of it, just as Jesus confirmed: "the Son of Man is Lord even of the sabbath" (Mark 2:28). Actually I could stop right here and we would have to conclude the biblical and qur'anic understandings of the sabbath are as similar as an igloo is to "I glue." They may look and sound alike, but that's all.

Next, Yahweh said the sabbath is a day in which no one, not even the stranger living among you, is to work at all. These two facts—Yahweh is the Lord of the sabbath and there is to be no work at all—are not part of the qur'anic description of sabbath.

There are five verses in the Qur'an that speak about the sabbath: Q2:65; 4:47, 154; 7:163; 16:124. Of the five sabbath verses, three pronounce judgment on those who break the sabbath (one verse even reminds the reader that Allah punished the Jews when he said, "Be ye apes"—and the Jews were graciously transformed into the lost tribe of Simian), and one verse warns the Jews to keep the sabbath without any specifications as to how, unlike Exodus 20:10. The last verse (16:124) is the most interesting: "The sabbath was only made (strict) for those who disagreed (as to its observance)." This verse is understood by Muslims and Muslim scholars to mean that Allah made the sabbath for only the Jews. The reason he made it so strict—although the Qur'an never mentions the strictures—is that the Jews were such a disagreeable lot. I suppose if I were a monkey I

---

items show how very different Allah is from Yahweh. It is only Yahweh who worked his sovereign will through a people (the Jews) with whom he made a covenant (promise). It is only in the Temple system established by Yahweh that we find the ultimate fulfillment of the great plan of God consummated in the incarnation of the final "Temple," Jesus. Allah and Yahweh share only one characteristic of which I'm aware: creator. After that, the similarity ends.

might be a bit ornery, too. In Table 5 below, I summarize the sabbath as understood by the Bible and the Qur'an.

Table 5. Comparison of sabbath in the Bible and Qur'an.

	Bible	Qur'an
Owner of the sabbath	God	Not mentioned
Emphasis	Rest	Not mentioned
Characteristics (Ex 20:10-11)	a) Seventh day b) It is holy and is to be kept holy c) God rested on the seventh day d) Blessed day	a) Not mentioned b) Not mentioned c) Not mentioned d) Not mentioned
Stipulation(s)	a) No one works b) Do not gather sticks (Nu 15:32ff)	a) Not mentioned b) Not mentioned
Judgment for breaking the commandment	Death (Ex 31:15)	Curse Simian-ization of Jews
Application of sabbath	Jew and stranger	Jews only

It seems to me there is only one conclusion that is possible from the facts of such a simple comparison. The qur'anic version of the fourth commandment, keeping the sabbath, is essentially not mentioned. And when reference is made to it, it doesn't seem to be the sabbath of the Bible.[5]

As for the sixth commandment, I believe it is doubtful to make a worthwhile comparison between it and its qur'anic partner. The murder of apostates is allowed in Islam; the life of Muhammad proved this to be true in many cases. There are also other occasions that seem to demand the murder of a person, but rather than enter a gray area, I am willing

---

5. I believe a more detailed examination of each of the "Ten Commandments" in the Qur'an would offer up the same result as this simple chart does for the sixth commandment. But this is a short introduction to the insider movement.

to allow the equivalency of the two commandments to stand as true. In the end, there is not hundred percent equivalence; it is only eighty-five percent at best. I wonder if Woodberry's exuberance to find a bridge or commonality between Islam and Christianity has not caused him to make an error in judgment?

MUHAMMAD: A SHAMELESS PLAGIARIST?

To approach Woodberry's conclusion about re-cooping the practices of Islam and making them Christian again (thus making it legitimate for Muslim Christians to remain in the Muslim context), it is best to examine his article on Islam's borrowing of Christian and Jewish religious forms.[6] It's there that he explains how he comes to an irenic view of Islam, that is, its parallelism to Judaism and Christianity. Once we understand his argument, the reasoning behind his notion that Paul might become a Muslim to Muslims will be clear.

Woodberry first traces the development of contextualization among Muslims beginning with John Wilder's 1977 article, "Some Reflections on Possibilities for People Movements Among Muslims." Perhaps this was a seed of IM, the germination of the idea that Messianic Judaism could be a model for Muslims. Contextualization's importance has grown, as evidenced by the many articles and books over the years since then.

Woodberry then discusses the reaction to the contextualization of Muslim forms. The Arab-speaking church expresses negativity to the use of Islamic language in Bible translation and any adaptation of Islamic forms for Christian worship. Woodberry even mentions the common objection from Muslims toward Christian contextualization of Islamic forms: deception.

Citing many sources that show how much Islam borrowed from or is simply similar to Judaism and Christianity (and which I am not citing for the sake of brevity), Woodberry believes this means Islam may be understood as "a contextualization for the Arabs . . . directly from Jews and Christians."[7] So according to Woodberry, Islam is really an Arab interpretation of Judeo-Christian monotheism for seventh century Arabia.

The five pillars of Islam are Woodberry's next topic. First he shows the similarity of the opening of the *shahada* ("I bear witness that there

---

6. Woodberry, "Contextualization," 171–86.
7. Ibid., 173.

is no god but Allah") to the *shema* (Deut 6:4). While Christians cannot recite the second part in which Muhammad is affirmed as Allah's messenger, the first half does give us some common ground.

The second pillar, salat, finds similarity in the actual word chosen (*salla*, the verb *to bow*) because it "had long been used for institutionalized prayer in synagogues and churches."[8] Woodberry also shows the preparations a Muslim makes for salat are similar to that of the Jews. These preparations include washing the entire body after certain bodily emissions have occurred, readying oneself for prayer with sand when water is not available, the direction of prayer (initially Muhammad received a revelation that Muslims shall pray toward Jerusalem, though this was later abrogated), and announcing one's intention to pray. Woodberry makes a case that the actual postures of salat came from Jewish and Christian forms; and then he addresses the similarities of salat's meanings and functions with Christian prayer. He approaches the subject in this way: salat has motifs Christians would be able to affirm and use in our own prayers. They include witness, the mercy of God, his sovereignty, and worship of God; finding refuge in God; seeking guidance and so on. Finally Woodberry includes a look at the mosque's borrowing of certain architectural features from churches and synagogues.

Zakat or almsgiving, the third pillar of Islam, is a word taken from Aramaic. Both the Qur'an and Bible encourage believers to give without ostentation, to have the proper attitude, and both mention God's reward for generosity.

The fourth pillar is *sawm* or fasting (especially during Ramadan). Fasting is important in all three monotheistic religions and while there are parallels, Woodberry suggests there are differences, too. For a Muslim, fasting is an act of obedience; it is a duty and a command from Allah. This is not the case (to the same degree) for the Christian. Furthermore, fasting is explicitly linked to forgiveness for the Muslim.

Hajj or pilgrimage to Mecca is the final pillar. It is important to note Woodberry's introduction to hajj: "Not too much attention will be given to the Pilgrimage since it was an adoption and reinterpretation of pagan rituals."[9]

---

8. Ibid., 175.
9. Ibid., 181.

After laying an extensive latticework of interconnection and parallelism, Woodberry delves into how Christians can reclaim and reuse the five pillars of Islam as Christian forms of worship. He does this by means of a case study. The details of the case study are far from compelling.[10] Why? While Woodberry keeps the location of the study anonymous (he never says why), I know he is speaking of the IM in Bangladesh. By doing so, if I may say with only the most respect for a great man of God who has been influential in the world of ministry to Muslims, the case study is make believe. No I don't mean Woodberry created it from whole cloth; however, according to eyewitness accounts of those who were at one time affiliated with the insider movements in Bangladesh, the entire movement is a creative charade of lies, shadows, and duplicity. Woodberry and many others have been hoodwinked by what they think they've seen.[11]

CONNECTING THE NON-CONNECTABLE

Woodberry's conclusions are worth noting. First he emphasizes the similarities of the Christian and Jewish forms to Islam's, but beyond the forms, he reminds us the functions are also close, thus allowing for the borrowing by Islam. He does caution us about "the problem of training leadership" and encourages the building of ties "to other segments of the church without inhibiting growth."[12] But the major problem is "how to reuse Muslim forms without retaining Muslim meanings"[13] and which can keep new believers from maturing.

There is little doubt about the credibility of Woodberry's case. The similarities of form and function exist between Islam, Judaism, and Christianity; however, I believe all this fine research begs the question: why should the forms be reused?

10. For a stark contrast, see Appendix 2, which *is* a compelling case study.

11. At the i2 Ministries' annual "IM: A Critical Assessment" conference of 2010 (held at Liberty University) and 2011 (Mt Vernon Baptist Church, Atlanta), we videotaped pastors and ex-insiders from Bangladesh who spoke to the falsification of numbers. The number of Muslim converts in Bangladesh has been cited as 300,000 or 500,000, and even as high as 1.2 million. These pastors, along with missionaries who are on the ground in Bangladesh, put the numbers at no more than 50,000—the most generous number they can give. Cf. Bill Nikides, "Interview with an ex-Insider" in *Chrislam*, 237. One former insider told me the number of insiders at present (2012) is less than 10,000 (personal correspondence).

12. Woodberry, "Contextualization," 181.

13. Ibid., 183.

I say it begs the question for two reasons. First he wraps up the theoretical with a case study—a case study that in reality doesn't exist. I'll speak to this below, but let me pose another question that must be answered before examining the similarities between the religions and their forms. Now remember, Woodberry wants to know if converts to Christianity can/should baptize Islamic forms in the process of their discipleship. He writes, "present formulations of Christian worship that utilize forms that are familiar to Muslims have arisen as Muslim converts have felt uncomfortable in existing churches and as evangelists have increasingly seen the variety of forms in which allegiance to Christ can be expressed."[14]

This is an understandable situation, one that I don't wish to minimize. So, given the circumstances of discomfort and a desire to worship God in ways that are meaningful, I understand Woodberry's desire to help converts from Islam.

DISCONNECTING ISLAM FROM CHRISTIANITY

I said that Woodberry's conclusion begs the question for two reasons. The second reason is that if we grant that the forms of Islam—the pillars—are borrowed forms, why would we reuse these forms knowing the nature of Islam? In other words, it all comes down to a theology of religions.

How do we see Islam? What is the nature of Islam? Is Islam just a collection of beliefs and rituals wrapped up in culture that is nice to study and think about? Is Islam simply a mixture of truth and error? Perhaps Islam is a kissing cousin to Judaism and Christianity? Just what should we think about Islam as a religion? I'm really asking this: what does the Bible say about religions that are not about Jesus?

1 Corinthians 9 is part of a larger context (chapters 8–10) in which Paul speaks to several matters of importance, one of them being the biblical view of the pagan religion practiced by the Corinthians. Paul writes, "we know that there is no such thing as an idol in the world" (1 Cor 8:4). We need to temper this statement with 1 Corinthians 10:20, "they sacrifice to demons and not to God." I understand Paul to mean that while the panoply of gods who inhabit the Greco-Roman pantheon exists in the worldview of the Corinthians, in reality they are nothing; they are not gods, but demons.

---

14. Ibid., 171.

Furthermore, Paul speaks to the seriousness of the demonic source of other religions. Consider 2 Corinthians 11:13–15: "For such men are false apostles, deceitful workers, disguising themselves as apostles of Christ. No wonder, for even Satan disguises himself as an angel of light. Therefore it is not surprising if his servants also disguise themselves as servants of righteousness, whose end will be according to their deeds."

If there are false apostles, they must have a false message. We would expect them to disguise themselves as counterfeits just as the father of all counterfeits, Satan, has disguised himself. These apostles are called Satan's servants. That can only mean they are wittingly or unwittingly used by Satan, and therefore their teachings are Satanic.

This is, I believe, an apt description of Islam—or any religion. This is a biblical view of other religions. Let me further illustrate the point by asking the question: Was Muhammad a prophet of Yahweh? My aim is to show you a false apostle as described in 2 Corinthians 11.

MUHAMMAD[15]

Carl Medearis, well known speaker, author, expert on Islam, and advocate of IM principles, writes, "It is important to consider that Muhammad was, at least, in the beginning, a man with a desire to discover God."[16] It's important to state that this is Medearis' view and not necessarily the view of all the other advocates of IM.[17] Medearis believes Muhammad desired to know God. So do Muslims. Let's examine this idea closely by suggesting the possibilities (a, b, c, and d) with their implications:

a. Muhammad desired to know God.

aa. So God fulfilled his desire and met him.

aaa. One implication is that Islam comes from God

b. Muhammad desired to know God.

bb. But God didn't fulfill his desire to meet him.

---

15. This section is adapted from my "The Lyrics of Carl Medearis: a Post-Modern Croons a Song of Cultural Imperialism" in *SFM* 7:4 (2011): 54–87; I've also reworked some material from "The Lyrics" for the section titled "The immaculate assumption?"

16. Medearis, "Muslims," 24.

17. It's important not to lump every advocate of the insiders movements into one massive pile on the question of Muhammad's prophethood; however, I know more than a few proponents of IM who do indeed see Muhammad favorably.

bbb. One implication is that Islam is not from God.

c. Muhammad did not desire to know God.

cc. But God met him despite his desire.

ccc. One implication is that Islam comes from God.

d. Muhammad did not desire to know God.

dd. So God fulfilled his desire and didn't meet him.

ddd. One implication is that Islam is not from God.

If Muhammad was sincere about knowing God and in fact knew God ("a" and "aa" above), the Qur'an must be scripture at some level; and Islam is therefore a true religion or at minimum, a religion with more truth than error. There are two possible stipulations for this:

- Perhaps Muhammad knew God but misunderstood God's communication resulting in a semi-inspired Qur'an. The Qur'an has truths that parallel the Bible, but it is not the fully revealed word of Yahweh. But there are too many unsolved mysteries surrounding the collection of the Qur'an and far too many contradictions between the Bible and the Qur'an to connect Yahweh to the Qur'an. This leads me to reject the idea that Muhammad knew Yahweh.
- Perhaps Muhammad knew God, but chose to be deceived by Gabriel, a supposed angel, in order to secure the opportunity of power and status in the Arabian Peninsula. If this scenario is true, Muhammad was a power-hungry maniac and the book he received was not from Yahweh.

If Muhammad was sincere, but God did not reveal himself ("bb"), this means Yahweh failed to answer a sincere prayer. Why would God not meet him? Why would God act in such a petulant manner? This scenario calls into question the character of the God of the Bible not Muhammad's character. I refuse to believe the notion that God would not hear the prayer of a sincere seeker for that is not the character of Yahweh. Therefore I must reject "b" as counter to what I know about Yahweh.

That leaves us "c" and "d." Here the common denominator is that Muhammad did not desire to know God (this was not Medearis' starting point, but it is mine). If God met Muhammad against the latter's wishes ("cc"), the Qur'an is a revelation of God, but we are still left with the contradictions between the Bible and the Qur'an. This impugns the very character of God. Is he a God who can speak diametrically opposed truths? But if Muhammad had no desire to meet God ("d")—and did not meet Yahweh ("dd")—this means Yahweh did not reveal Islam. But Islam had to come from somewhere. That leaves us with the one possible solution: the source of Islam is the angel of light (2 Cor 11:14).

Is Muhammad a prophet of Yahweh? I don't see how he could be. And if he is not a prophet of Yahweh, he is a prophet of the angel of light. There is no other option given to us by scripture. Is Islam a religion we can play with, taking bits and pieces and fiddling with it as if it were a tinker toy? I don't believe the Bible takes this view of other religions. The source of Muhammad's revelation was either his very fertile imagination or the angel of light.

I have already conceded that the forms of Islam were borrowed from Judaism and Christianity, but what I cannot concede is that the forms are now separable from Islam or redeemable due to the irreconcilable problem that Islam has a demonic source.[18]

MBB'S

Just as Woodberry's article ended with a suspicious case study, I want to end this chapter with my own dubious case study—that is, I made it up. I will let you decide which of the two case studies is credible.

Suppose you come from a Mormon home. You are raised to believe in the gospel of Mormonism, understanding Jesus as Satan's brother, heavenly father as an exalted human although having supernatural abilities and powers, and the Church of the Latter Day Saints to be the true restored church of Jesus Christ. One day you are introduced to the real gospel and real Jesus and eventually place your faith and trust in him. You begin attending a typical evangelical church but notice some things about it that make you uncomfortable. You decide to gather some like-minded converts and create an insider fellowship of MBBs, Mormon Background Believers.

What forms from the Mormon Church will you baptize and reuse? You are uncomfortable with what you experienced with the First Church of Mayberry. You are looking for a way to express your new faith in a manner to which you are accustomed. And after all, since much of the

---

18. I develop this in "IM: Inappropriate Missiology" in *Chrislam*, 141–43.

LDS form was borrowed from Protestant churches, you figure you'll re-borrow the forms.

So, you decide you will no longer meet with other Protestants, but only with the MBBs. You stick with the hymns you learned as a child; they're comforting and full of theology that you are in the process of changing to match biblical theology. You are still undecided about the LDS scriptures; you are still reading them and enjoying them though you do sense you may eventually stop reading the texts. You maintain your sacramental undergarments, baptism of the dead (since there is some support, not strong you realize, but some support from the Bible), and a Christianized notion of the Aaronic priesthood.

One day you invite several family members who are still LDS to join your insider worship. When they arrive and observe your small fellowship, some are willing to share their observations and questions with you.

"I'm confused. Are you an apostate or LDS?" asks the first.

One of your less confused relatives says, "Why are you trying to trick us into thinking you are LDS? What are you trying to do?" He stomps off quite angry.

The case study is make believe, but the parallels to Woodberry's case study are not. When Muslims encounter insiders—Muslim followers of Jesus or Messianic Muslims—they think the insiders are trying to hoodwink them into thinking they are Muslims. No one likes to be made a fool, especially when it comes to religion.[19] In the case of Islam, it can result in violence.

Reuse the forms of Islam? Who are we trying to kid? Islam is not just another religion; everything about it is anti-Christian, anti-Trinity, anti-Father, anti-Son, anti-church, anti-cross, and anti-Bible. With all those anti's it is time to say "Uncle!"

---

19. The following is part of an email describing Muslims who follow Jesus but remain as Muslims. I have dropped all names and changed some of the wording in order to maintain anonymity for the author, but notice the *result* of being an insider: "As you know one of our brothers was snatched for money, but is now released. I am fortunate to have spent a few days with him. He has really been through the wringer; he's suffered quite a bit. Why? Was it because he wanted to avoid persecution, hiding while being an *insider*? No. Was it because he compromised his faith with Islam? No. Was it because he accommodated his language to Islam in order to make Muslims happy? No. In fact, it was mostly because he was *inside* and Muslims could easily see what he was about. Muslims believed their foundations were *threatened* by someone on the *inside*."

11

Conversion Doesn't Mean to Put a Suit on a Frog

THE PREVIOUS EIGHT CHAPTERS have examined the IM advocates' assumptions about Islam in the light of the scriptures. The goal has been to understand what the Bible says about our view of other religions. In this chapter I am concerned with the third assumption mentioned in chapter one: the understanding of conversion from the IM perspective. I want to first examine the idea of religion as it interacts with conversion. Then we will turn to the assumption of IM about conversion, followed by a look at what the Bible has to say about conversion.

WINE, WOMEN AND BACON

Epistrephō, to turn, is not a problematic word for the proponents of IM, for they agree that the heart must be changed by new birth in Jesus. The rub between the advocates of IM and its critics is how it all takes place. By this I mean that those who advocate for IM believe the manner in which insiders are converting, then remaining within Islam, maintains the integrity of the gospel. But that's not all, for there are other proponents that believe it is fairly typical of the critics—like me—who squeeze the new followers of Jesus through the Western sieve of conversion, making them *Christians* (here I'm using the word pejoratively). Although those who mold Muslim converts into *Christians* may mean well, the proponents of IM believe we are really harming the converts by insisting they call themselves *Christians*—even though *Christian* may mean a wine-drinking, woman-chasing, pork-eating idolater—extracting the new follower of Jesus from their culture—even though they ought to remain within their situation—pushing them into the local church that may be hostile to ex-Muslims, rather than helping them enter the kingdom of God without our trappings of *Christianity*. When missionaries do these kinds of things to converts, the implication is that missionaries are actually harming the integrity of the gospel.

RELIGION: A FOUR-LETTER WORD?

Before I get to the discussion of conversion a few words must be said concerning *religion*, one of the topics that contributes to how we understand conversion. We Christians do not think of ourselves as religious. We tend to think of religion as a man-made contraption that we must shun. After all, our relationship to Jesus is all about him; it's not a religion, but a relationship. I know we've already had this discussion, but there's just a bit more that needs saying.

The word *religion* is believed to come from the Latin *religare*, meaning to bind together. The idea may be that religion is a duty, something to which we are bound and obligated. My question here is this: do any of us believe we have no obligations to Jesus? Are we not bound to him, owing him our gratitude, worship, and love? These are rightly called religious duties or obligations. Let me say it again: religion is not a four-letter word. It is true that following Jesus is a matter of heart allegiance. We are Christians not because we join a local congregation and show up for worship on Sundays. That's the religion part, right? Nevertheless, if we are honest with ourselves and with the word *religion* itself, there are aspects of our relationship with Jesus that are religious; we do things a certain way because of our religion.

A great example of Jesus' approach to religion is seen in his discussion with the Samaritan woman. She was an adherent of another religion. When he said to her that "salvation is from the Jews" (John 4:22), was he telling her that Judaism was no different, no truer, no better than her own religion? Actually Jesus made a bold declaration about Judaism, true Judaism: it was the only religion in which one finds salvation. This is my first conclusion about religion: it is true that salvation is in Jesus, but Jesus emphasizes salvation is only in the Jesus of Jesus-centered Judaism, not the Jesus of Hinduism (an avatar of Vishnu), Buddhism (a wise sage), Mormonism (the spirit brother of Lucifer), Jehovah's Witness (a second level god) or Islam (merely a prophet to the Jews).

Jesus' view of religion appears to include the idea that one religion can be better than another, that the religion of the Jews has something no other religion does. That's pretty bold of Jesus; he's making a value statement about two religions. If Jesus were working in our modern world, he's just opened himself up to possible sensitivity training due to his lack of tolerance. I wonder how the God of the universe would handle sensitivity training? I'd pay to sit through that!

I need to be careful here. While affirming the importance of Judaism, it seems to me Jesus is not calling the woman to become a first century Jew, but he is calling her to himself, the embodiment of authentic Judaism. He did not give her a tract with the Seven Jewish Spiritual Laws that concludes with the sinner's prayer. It is clear he was not interested that she become a Jew when he said to her: "an hour is coming, and now is, when the true worshipers will worship the Father in spirit and truth; for such people the Father seeks to be His worshipers" (4:23). It's the Father who does the seeking for worshippers. These worshippers will be both Jew and gentile, and yes, even Samaritan. But the worship takes place "in spirit and truth" as opposed to *in* Judaism. At that moment in time, the Judaism expressed in the life of Jesus was truly the religion of salvation; that is, it was the religious expression of God's universal intent to bring light to the nations through the nation of Israel as they encountered God's suffering servant (cf. Isa 42:1–6; 49:5–6; 60:3).

There were certainly times in his ministry when Jesus showed great disdain for bad religion and those who were religiously bad (Matt 12:25–29, 37–39; 16:12; 22:29–32; 23:1–39), though this was not one of those moments. But Jesus was not ashamed to make the point to the woman at the well that the Messiah, the one even she a Samaritan hoped for, came from within the Jewish religion and context, rather than the Samaritan religion. He helped her understand there is a true religion and that the practice of her religion fell short of what he offered. So this is my second conclusion about religion: there is one true religion and every other religion is false religion.

Jesus did not have a pluralistic view of religions; he was an exclusivistic Jew. He inaugurated the kingdom of God through his practice of Judaism—yes, through religion. His first sermon was, "The kingdom of God is at hand" (Mark 1:15). The act of preaching is a quintessentially religious behavior. The Judaism that Jesus practiced was the relationship-oriented religion experienced by Abraham who, though not a Jew, was reckoned righteous by faith (Gen 15:6). It was the Judaism of Isaiah, the missionary religion of light for the nations (Isa 42:6). Jesus lived Jeremiah's Judaism, the religion of a new heart and covenant (Jer 31:31–3). It was the Judaism of the prophet Joel in which God called for a holy fast, another ritual of religion (1:13–14). Jesus inaugurated and lived out the kingdom in his ministry by practicing authentic biblical Judaism. Therefore, my third conclusion about religion is that Jesus did not think of religion as a four-letter word.

What does any of this have to do with conversion? When discussing conversion from an insider movement perspective, as you will see, *Christianity* is thought to be a religion into which critics of insider movements bring new converts. The proponents of IM wish to see converts enter the kingdom of heaven without converting into *Christianity*. Part of the problem is that we the critics and proponents of IM are using *Christianity* differently. But there's more under the surface not being said. So let's examine this more closely.

CONVERSION OR CHRISTIANIZATION?

In offering four suggestions that help us "emphasize the gospel, not religious conversion"[1]—meaning conversion to Christianity—Rebecca Lewis suggests this: "If well-meaning Christians tell seekers that they must come to God not just through Christ but also through Christianity, help the Christians understand this requirement is 'not in line with the truth of the gospel' (Galatians 2:14–21, 3:6–9,14, 5:6, 6:12–16; Ephesians 3:6; First Corinthians 7:17–19; Colossians 2:16–23, Acts 10 and 15)."[2]

Lewis' other three suggestions offer the same sort of advice: interested Muslims don't need to join a Christian group to be saved; some Christians have taught that Jesus is the savior of Christians rather than savior of the world; and some Christians teach the road to Christ must go through Christianity. Are missionaries dishonoring the gospel by making Muslim followers of Jesus *join the church*, thus extracting themselves from their local contexts and becoming part of a structure that is often hostile to Muslim converts? Are we making new converts from Islam enter *Christianity* as the advocates of IM understand it? Do new believers

---

1. Lewis, "Insider Movements," 19.
2. Ibid., 19.

become *Christians* in the worst sense of the word; that is, do they leave the non-pork eating religion of Islam only to become pork-eating *Christians*?

This view of Christianity is one that is sympathetic to how most Muslims view our religion. Imagine meeting a Muslim for the first time. He asks you about your religion. You tell him you are a Christian.

He lowers his gaze and shakes his head slowly, saying, "Is it true you only pray at meals, never fast, eat pork, drink wine, and then on Sundays you make it all go away with a few words of confession?"

How will you answer him? Most proponents of IM suggest this approach: "I am a follower of Jesus. What you have described is not what I am." I suggest something similar, but the word *Christian* doesn't scare me: "I am a Christian, but what you've described is not my religion. My religion teaches me that Jesus is the Messiah who died on the cross, conquering death. My religion teaches me that because he rose from the dead, so that I will live forever with him."

It's painful to point out the differences in the approaches above. The first is less concerned with sharing the gospel with a Muslim than it is with appearing *not* to be, you know, one of that type of *Christian*. The second approach is focused on using the misconceptions about *Christian* as a means of sharing Christ. The first answer is defensive; the second is bold.

Just as religion is not a four-letter word, neither is Christianity. Because Muslims mischaracterize our religion does not mean I don't want to be known as a Christian; rather it provides me an opportunity to let them know what a real Christian looks like. Why do we missionaries let *Christianity* remain a curse word? The religion of Christianity is not something of which I am ashamed. It is in fact, the religion of the authentic Jesus. Biblical Christianity proclaims Jesus. Jesus' followers and disciples today are called Christians and they practice Christianity.

So for the sake of our discussion about conversion, Christianity is the religion into which one is converted. Whether one likes it or not, the reality is that anyone who follows Jesus is a Christian. A Christian is a member of the Body of Christ. Most of the proponents of IM use Christianity as a pejorative, sympathetic to how Muslims understand it. There is some validity to the viewpoint, but the reaction is what concerns me. When Muslims denigrate *Christianity* they mock a hollow, superficial shell of my religion. And when new believers come out of Islam, they do not become *Christians* as the Muslim describes them, but real Christians: Bible-reading, Jesus-loving (and probably non pork-eating) Christians.

SET THEORY RESET

Let's go a bit deeper than mere definition of words. Carl Medearis corroborates Lewis' view of conversion when he writes, "When we preach Christianity, we find all these things on our plate [the Crusades, Protestants vs. Catholics, persecution of scientists, etc.]. . . . I believe that the gospel and the religion of Christianity can be two different messages. Even opposed on some points. When we preach Christianity, we have to own it. When we preach Jesus, we don't have to own anything. Jesus owns us."[3]

Perhaps the most egregious thing we Christians do, according to Medearis, is that we may be preaching the wrong message. "We're busy trying to find the boundary line that separates the saved from the unsaved and trying to bring people across that boundary by convincing them to think like we do."[4]

At the heart of Medearis' statement—the assumption that drives his view—is the bounded and centered set theory. You've probably never heard of set theory, but we missionaries love to discuss it and even include a figure or two to accompany it in our articles and books; it just makes us look a little bit smarter when we do. Well, not being above making myself look smart, I have included it as a picture as well. Bounded and centered sets are concepts taken from mathematics, applied to social groups by anthropologist Paul Hiebert, and then often misapplied to conversion by some of the advocates of the insider movements and the emergent church. Medearis has misapplied it, too.

So let me show you where I think the problem is—I mean other than the fact that the proponents of IM don't really exegete scripture—rather *they more often than not rely on the social sciences for their conclusions.* Set theory is another example of just that.

Bounded Set

The bounded set (Figure 2) is simply the idea that a boundary exists between those who are in the set and everyone else. Hiebert was describing communities that are closed and static; their boundaries make membership clear. You are either *in* or *out*. The Masons are an example of a bounded set. They have explicit membership rules along with rituals and rites that maintain a sense of solidarity and cohesion.

---

3. Medearis, *Speaking*, 47.
4. Ibid., 48.

Figure 2. The bounded set.

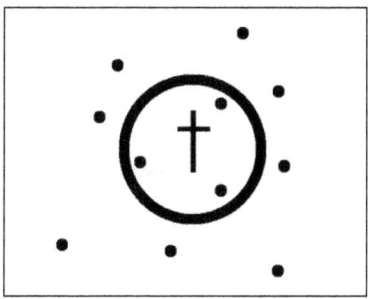

When the bounded set is applied to the church, especially in light of what it means to be saved, the bounded set is thought to be static rather than dynamic, exclusive as opposed to inclusive, and most importantly for Medearis, represents the vast majority of evangelicals' understanding of salvation, the gospel, church, and Christianity. He writes: "This diagram represents the idea of salvation many of us have. We live in the circle and to bring others inside of it, we have to convince them to adopt our beliefs. We typically use the word *confession* to describe the act when someone self-narrates his or her change of heart. . . . When we point at the boundary, we're trying to define it. But if Jesus is lifted up, *He* draws people to Himself. It isn't our job to lose sleep trying to decide if so-and-so is 'in' or 'out.'"[5]

Obviously Medearis is not enamored with the bounded set though he does see its value: "I'm not saying there isn't a point at which people genuinely come into the kingdom."[6] Yet he advises us, "Throw the circle away!"[7] Why? "If we're saved into the boundaries of a circle, we owe our allegiance to that boundary, and we're going to try to bring others inside it."[8] As Medearis sees it then, the problem with the church as a bounded set—salvation means you're *in* or *out*—is that we make the most important thing the line, the boundary, and the border because it provides us some sense of cohesion. That line is churchianity and not Jesus. Medearis thinks most evangelicals are emphasizing the line rather than the Savior.

---

5. Ibid., 63, 67.
6. Ibid., 71.
7. Ibid.
8. Ibid., 74.

Do you hear the echo of Lewis' previous statement in Medearis' words? We don't save people into *Christianity*—as if we, the non-IMers, were trying to do that anyway.

Centered Set

There is another perspective: the centered set. The centered set is ideologically based. It is less concerned with membership than it is with a center or essential cohesive ideology or doctrine that binds people together. The Democratic and Republican political parties here in the U.S. illustrate centered sets. Neither party has strict membership rules that keep a person in one party or the other. Membership is voluntary and ideologically based. A person becomes a Democrat because he values government help for the poor or paying teachers better salaries; or one becomes a Republican because she values lower taxes or making government smaller. A Democrat may vote for a Republican, and vice versa, precisely because there are no hard and fast boundaries that make one either *in* or *out* of a particular political party.

Medearis believes the centered set best describes how we should view the church and salvation . In the centered set, the ideology that brings cohesion is represented by a cross in the center; and in this case it represents Jesus. Jesus is the focus of our attention. It doesn't matter who's *in* or *out* because that's not the question. The real issue is this: Am I moving to or away from Jesus? Those who are moving toward Jesus are in relationship with him and there is no boundary to worry about, no *in* or *out*.

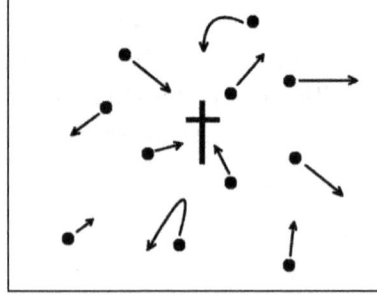

Figure 3. Centered Set

Sounds good doesn't it? It's nice to get out from under the restrictions of boundaries and borders, the artificial lines drawn in the sand of a beach we do not even own. Catchy and emotionally satisfying, yes; but is it biblically accurate?[9]

Bounded-Centered Set

I believe there is an integrated, more holistic way of looking at salvation, the gospel, church, Christianity, and being saved (Figure 4). Following Medearis' footsteps, let me mistakenly apply the bounded-centered set to something it was never meant to explain.

Figure 4. The bounded-centered set: both are true.

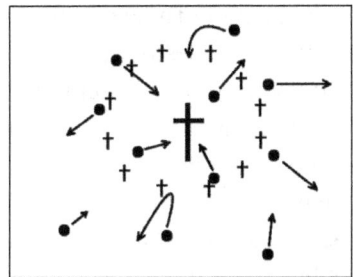

Here the boundary is actually Jesus himself; that is, he is the circle of crosses (use your imagination to think of it as a solid line). Jesus as a boundary is, believe it or not, biblical: "I am the way, the truth, the life" (John 14:6; cf. Acts 4:12; Rom 10:9–10). He is the line drawn in the sand and in fact, even the beach is his! This bounded-centered set has as its boundary—a necessity for identification—the covenantal relationship Jesus offers. The boundary is Jesus, not Christianity or something manmade—as Medearis and some others of the IM believe we think. There does come a time when the follower of Jesus admits, confesses, prays, cries out, weeps, states (or all the above): "Jesus is Lord." There is content to knowing Jesus; that is, in order to know Jesus (relationship part), there must be some knowledge of who he is (the content part).

9. It's interesting that many who espouse the emergent church movement take up the centered set as the model for church in the twenty-first century. I am neither opposed to the centered set nor to the bounded set as models, but my question is why one or the other? In fact, my real question is to ask, does this model actually help us do the preaching of the gospel, church planting and discipleship? Or does it get in the way by creating some interesting discussions that generally create more division than they do unity? That would make, ironically, those of us who argue over the bounded-centered set part of bounded set because you either agree or disagree (another way of saying either *in* or *out*). Sorry, I just misapplied the theory again. See how easy it is to do that?

The content of the ministry, character, personality, and nature of Jesus is the line in the sand.

Conversely there is nothing biblical about following Jesus without the revelation/understanding of who he is. There is nothing biblical about having the wrong Jesus: i.e., Muslim 'Isa. Just because one says, "I follow Jesus" or "I love Jesus" does not a Christian make. A lemon is not a lemon because it is yellow and pulpy—so are the yellow pages—but because it has the DNA of lemondom. The lemon has lemon-content; the follower of Jesus has Jesus-content, Messiah-DNA, and the essence of Christ.

Some of us call our "border crossing" (breaking into the circumference of that bounded set) being born again; others speak of confession; some talk of being a follower of Jesus; still others might say a formal prayer or a promise to obey him in addition to their baptism. All this is indicative of the bounded set, a necessary component of knowing and following Jesus. Once the Ethiopian eunuch understood of whom the prophet Isaiah wrote, he made a run for the border by asking for baptism; he understood the Messiah had come and was Jesus himself! He became part of the bounded set by crossing the line, although he didn't know it.

But Jesus is more than just a boundary; he is also the focus and the goal of entering the bounded set. He is our ideology. This too is biblical ("Follow me," Matt 4:19; Mark 8:34; Luke 9:59; John 1:43). Notice that some within the bounded-centered set (of Figure 5) are not moving toward Christ—they are not maturing—while others are moving away from Jesus. We call this backsliding. Still others are moving toward him, which is maturity, sanctification, and discipleship. Others outside the set are moving to or away from Jesus. Both the bounded and the centered sets are true; neither is a complete picture of what is happening in the church because of Jesus. Ironically, missiologists already know that both sets are of equal value, but those who wish to be edgy shine their light on one set or the other. This is a mistake. Consider Roger Chapman's wise observation: "The hard work for the missionary begins after baptizing the converts, i.e., they must be instructed in all the teachings of Christianity. Applying to missions the centered set method for categorization would shift the emphasis from baptizing to discipling, from the converting of individuals to the nurturing of corporate bodies. The bounded set fits conversion but not maturation. The centered set fits maturation but not conversion. Church planting, not just the converting of individuals, was the method of the apostle Paul (Allen 1962:81); in other words, *the bounded set should be accompanied by the centered set*"[10] (emphasis mine).

Rebounding

My concern with Medearis' picture is not that he's wrong, because he's right! I mean that if we make artificial boundaries in order to distinguish who's *in* or *out*, we are certainly not preaching the gospel. But when we point to Jesus, he is *both the focus* and *the boundary*. I know Medearis agrees; I just wish he had said it.

Having purposely misapplied the bounded and centered set theory to salvation, let me apply in a better way: to the church. What is the church? Is it an organization of people or is it an organism that is headed by Jesus? The answer is, of course, yes and yes.

It is an organization. Many of the biblical words used to describe the church connote some type of organization: elders, deacons, apostles, prophets, prophetesses and so on. Paul tells us to pray for the leaders of the local church; this is part of the organizational dimension of the church; therefore it seems quite likely that the bounded set works well with this perspective.

On the other hand, the church is also an organism whose head is Christ. The New Testament uses terms that speak of the relationship the church has to Christ as a living thing: the bride of Christ, the body of Christ, living stones, and the list continues. This fits well with the unbounded or centered set, which speaks of discipleship and movement toward Jesus as one's Savior and friend.

BIBLICAL CONVERSION

Now we come to the real heart of conversion: what does the Bible say? Let's leave behind the social science that can gum up our thinking. Is conversion simply putting a suit on a frog? Is conversion more than an outward change, more than a change in religious affiliation?[11]

10. Chapman, "Cognitive Categories."

11. I would be surprised if you were aware of a little known fractured fairy tale about a witch who turns a prince into a frog. The prince could only become human again if he wore a little prince suit, wished over and over that he were a prince again, and even with all that, the most beautiful princess in the land would have to kiss him. So he wears the suit and wishes the wish, but he remains a frog. Neither the suit nor the wishing make his dream come true. Eventually the most beautiful princess in the land does kiss the

Conversion is a turning, with an implication of *turning to* and *turning from*. The sinner turns to the Savior and in doing so, turns from that which previously held his attention. Do we embrace Jesus only to hold on to our past life of being a serial murderer? Do we begin following Jesus but not turn from our secular materialism? Are we called to be Christians who love Jesus and become members of his Body, only to maintain our memberships in the Ku Klux Klan, the Mafia, Satanism, the worship of the goddess Diana—or even keeping our membership in AARP?

This turning, this *epistrephō*, is found throughout the New Testament. Here's just a partial list of the things from which one turns at conversion:

- Acts 3:26, from wicked ways
- James 5:20, from the error of one's way
- Acts 26:18, from darkness to light, from Satan to God
- Acts 14:15, from things of no value to the living God
- 1 Thessalonians 1:9, from idols to the living God
- 1 Peter 2:25, from going astray and turning to the Shepherd

Why wouldn't we expect a conversion from Islam to have the same elements: a turning from Islam and a turning to the Savior; and a turning from a religion of bondage coupled with a turning to the one who brings freedom and life? But in fact, some of the advocates of IM do not seem expect that. What do they expect to see?

Figure 5 illustrates my interpretation of how some of the advocates of IM understand conversion. When a Muslim first hears the preaching of the gospel (A), he is not yet a follower of Jesus. Islam is still sufficient for him; it is a complete way of life. Somewhere along the way he comes to Jesus, recognizing his own inability to be good enough to please God (B) because the Father has revealed this to him. When the decision is finally made to follow Jesus, the result is a Muslim who loves Jesus (C). He retains the socio-religious "suit" of Islam but at the core of his identity and allegiance is Jesus. It looks like he has a Muslim veneer to the new inner man.

---

smartly-sartorial-wishing-upon-a-wish-frog-prince, but he does not turn into a prince. The princess immediately changes into a frog! The moral of the story is, of course, why would anyone believe a witch? Or, conversion is more than skin deep.

Figure 5. The IM model of conversion.

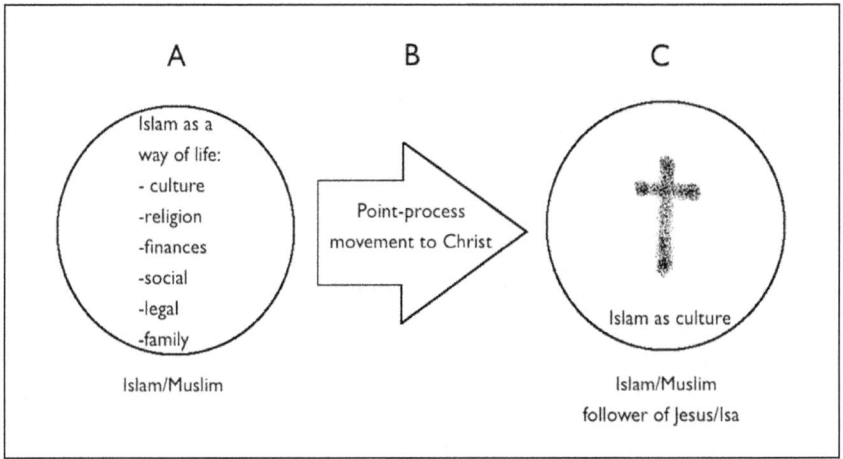

There is a problem with this model. We can see the *turning to*, but where is the *turning from*? What's really happened, though you can't see it, is occurring in the movement to Christ. Inside the arrow (B), Islam is slowly morphing from a complete way of life (culture, religion, finances, etiquette, etc.) into an incomplete way of life. In other words, inexplicably Islam transmogrifies from a womb to an appendage; from a way of life to a heritage. It appears the IM understanding of conversion is a turning to Jesus and a partial turning from Islam. Is a partial turning from Islam a conversion? Isn't it really just a partial turning to Jesus? Aren't we really seeing a frog in a suit? Isn't this syncretistic?

I believe it is biblical to see the circle of Islam not morphed into something new, but vanish altogether. Islam is part of the bondage and prison that once held the believer. The religion of Muhammad demands enslavement to worship a God one cannot ever know; in fact, the God of Islam deliberately keeps himself from being known. The religion of Muhammad is actualized or made relevant to the slaves of Allah by the prophet's example. It is an example that includes killing those who recited poetry that satirized him, or the killing of 900 Jews in one day.[12] Why would we encourage new believers to remain in such a prison?

---

12. For these examples and more from the life of Muhammad, see A. Guillaume. *The Life of Muhammad: A Translation of Isḥāq's Sīrat Rasūl Allāh*. Karachi, Pakistan: Oxford University Press. 1955.

SOME QUESTIONS

In this chapter on conversion I've shown how the assumption of the advocates of IM plays out in the life of a convert. The new convert remains in Islam as a Messianic Muslim or Muslim follower of Jesus. Since conversion through the church or Christianity is unnecessary, even unbiblical according to advocates of IM, the new believer's environment remains the same, although his heart has turned to Jesus.

On the other hand, biblical conversion is nothing like the proponents of IM suggest. It is a turning to Jesus and a turning from a religion that is demonically sourced. The DNA of Islam is nothing like that of Christianity. Placing the nucleus of one species into the egg of another does not necessarily produce something better; rather it brings about a hybrid. Christian faith implanted into the form of Islam does not give birth to true Christian faith and practice, but it does produce something different. And if it's different than Christian faith, it is not Christian.

What is the connection of these insiders to the visible church at large? How are they discipled as followers of Jesus when they are effectively Muslim? These and other questions are the serious problems that arise when we disciple new believers in Jesus to keep the shackles of Islam on one's heart and mind.

12

Biblically Incredible or Incredibly Brilliant?

I HAVE PRETTY MUCH introduced you to the entire arsenal of scriptures that serve as the foundation for the insider movements. I have tried to limit the discussion to the three assumptions introduced at the very beginning. Let me first summarize what I believe are the most important conclusions a study of scriptures shows about IM, then I want to follow this with some practical implications.

FOUR REMARKS

1. *What is the nature of religion, especially Islam?* It is hard to see from the passages we've looked at that God works in other religions. Admittedly, there is some ambiguity in several passages, but as the proponents attempt to lay out their case for IM, it's difficult to see how ambiguity sitting in the mortar of the silence of scripture creates a strong foundation for anything but trouble. On the one hand it is not biblically justifiable to say Islam is a religion that rebels against God (Kevin Higgins stated this previously), yet on the other to believe Yahweh overcomes the demonic nature of Islam (again, as Higgins believes) in order to establish relationships with its adherents. I don't understand how suggesting God's supposed willingness to work in other religions enhances his graciousness and mercy when it actually cheapens what God has accomplished in the incarnation. IM is not a rediscovery of the incarnation; it is a misappropriation of it.

2. *What is a relationship with Yahweh?* We evangelicals are in love with the word *relationship*. We seem to think it pretty much captures the essence of who we are and who Yahweh is. I am not cautioning against the use of the word or the concept; however, it does seem prudent not to jump to conclusions when we see something we may not understand. Let's all take a deep breath and realize that our relationship with Yahweh is based on what we've seen in scripture, on his character, and on his mercy—not on our observations.

3. *Can a theology of religions find its basis in the social sciences?* The scriptures should inform our anthropological observations and reports from the field. If anthropology plays an inordinate role in funding our understanding of the scriptures, the result may be an ad hoc type of theology. Why would we let the social sciences re-craft—I almost wrote *re-Kraft*—the biblical narrative to fit what we see happening? The answer is that we should not. A theology of religions properly based upon the scriptures is not a minor doctrine we can afford to ignore just because it may be cumbersome, politically incorrect and apparently discriminatory. A proper theology of religions touches every major area of theology, but primarily missions, the incarnation, inspiration of the scriptures, ecclesiology, soteriology (I lied when I told you this word would not appear again; sorry).

4. *Is this just a discussion about vocabulary?* In the background of what we've discussed is the nagging thought that has perhaps popped up several times: "This sounds like semantics." Sometimes I'm tempted to believe that, too. But the idea that it's all just semantics comes from laziness or perhaps the refusal to think through the observations, to work through the articles, and to study the scriptures. The disagreements over what the critics of IM and its advocates believe about the insider movements goes to the heart of how we understand scripture, how we handle and interpret scripture, the way we understand religions, and how we disciple new converts. No, this is not simply a matter of semantics—I'm convinced I'm right and advocates are sure they are. Our views are diametrically opposed at certain points.

A GOOD STEWARD

There will be other books and articles to come that will, I trust, dig deeper and develop more thoroughly the issues mentioned here. I am sure I haven't answered every question and adequately met each objection, but I am firmly convinced insider movements do not withstand biblical scrutiny. IM may stand unfazed by this study, continuing because these kinds of things often have a life of their own. In fact, it's hard to deny what one has seen and experienced as the advocates tell us. After all, a missionary with a story always sounds more intriguing (and more convincing?) than a missionary who expounds scripture. My study of scripture and my ministry among Muslims leads me to conclude that the scriptures are either silent about, ambiguous toward, or simply do not support IM's assertions.

There is little doubt about my bias. I stated up front my position, but it is not a position that is based on the idea that I don't like those involved in the IM. In fact, I know quite a few of those who hold opposing opinions to mine. I genuinely like them. So there is no animus or grudge-holding in my position. I am not driven to my position because I've been hurt, offended, attacked or maligned. I just want to be faithful to scripture.

I am convinced from scripture—not from reason or logic—that insider movements are not brilliantly incredible. It is my conviction that IM is theologically misinformed, using the Bible as a proof-text for support of Western missionary observations.

So now what? I think the answer is painfully obvious. I don't mean to be sarcastic by saying this. What I mean to say is that I think the answer to IM will hurt; it will take an emotional toll if you do what I am about to suggest.

First, what do you do if you don't believe I've represented the IM position fairly or that I've played around with the scriptures? I am open to discussion on these points. I have a blog. I regularly visit www.biblicalmissiology.org, write articles for St Francis Magazine, and I have even been known to answer letters. I welcome comments, criticisms, and honest discussion about these matters.

Second, what do you do if the things I've written make sense and express what you believe to be a fair, honest, and accurate representation of the scriptures? There are a number of things you could do.

You might want to begin your own investigation about mission organizations you support. Peppered throughout the book are names of some of these organizations. Where do the organizations you support stand on the issues of IM, dual identity, remaining in Islam, etc.? Be prepared to hear answers that dance around the clarity you seek. Most mission organizations that minister to Muslims know about insider movements; they also know whether or not they have missionaries involved in them. While many mission organizations *do* have an opinion about IM, fewer have written policies about it, and there is only a microscopic number of missions that actively enforce the policy. It's my opinion the policies are not enforced because moribund bureaucraticization has taken over in many mission organizations; that is, policies are believed to be sufficient to correct and guide behavior. But humans, even we the redeemed, rankle at authority figures telling us what to think and what to do. Mission organizations are made up of missionaries; and frankly, some the most stubborn characters I've ever met are missionaries. Herding cats or getting toothpaste back in the tube is easier than getting a group of missionaries to go in the same direction or take correction.

If you support missionaries who work in a Muslim, Hindu, or Buddhist context, perhaps it's time to begin a conversation with them. Where do they come down on the issues I've discussed? An interesting question to pursue with them is to ask if they have written about their experiences and if so, have they have used a pen name—and why. You may have noticed one pen name in this book; perhaps what you don't know is the surprising number of missionaries who do write with a pen name—ostensibly for security—but not even their supporters are aware of the identity behind the nom de plume. *Don't let your missionary hide behind a pen name while holding views you and your church do not support.*

What should you do if you discover missionaries you support are on the opposite side of the issues as you? This is where the emotional and financial toll kicks in. You've trusted and loved your missionaries for many years. You've learned from them; you pray for them; they've been in your home. Now you have learned something that disturbs you. What do you do?

"Faithful are the wounds of a friend, but deceitful are the kisses of an enemy" (Prov 27:6). Scripture enjoins us to steer away from deceit. Letting your annoyance, puzzlement, anger or whatever the emotion you are feeling fester will not bring clarity, change, healing, and a clear conscience. If you come to a point of impasse, that is, you believe one thing and the missionary you support believes another, well, it's not *your* money that supports them. God has made you a steward of *his* funds. So you are to decide as a steward or manager if this is the best, most proper use of God's resources. God is not going to decide for you. Don't throw out a fleece. A fleece never corrects syncretism; and in fact, putting out a fleece may actually be an act of cowardice (unlike the fleece of Gideon). Either what I've said makes sense or it doesn't. You either agree, disagree, or need to investigate for yourself.

Above all I encourage you to come to a decision about this important matter of insider movements. Deciding not to decide because it's painful is a decision to allow the problem to worsen. This is not a peripheral issue that affects only a few people. This is not just petty verbal jousting among missionaries. There are eternal ramifications for our choices, for our opinions, and for our teachings. It takes a person with a real spine to make a stand, knowing friends and colleagues may be annoyed (at best) or ostracized (at worst). Stand on the courage of your convictions. Be honest in your friendships. Remain faithful to scripture.

Appendix 1

Rev. Bassam Madany writes, "During the second half of the twentieth century, a paradigm shift began taking place in Western missionary organizations. With some an uncritical adoption of cultural anthropology as a methodological tool for doing missionary work was taking root. Former methods revolved around the final authority of an inerrant scripture as a starting point of mission work. The new method was discussed in a paper read at a meeting of concerned missionaries at the Four Brooks Conference Center in Bucks County, Pennsylvania, in July, 1985."

A STATEMENT OF MISSIONARY CONCERN

As a result of the spread of a new theory of missions known as Contextualization among many Evangelicals, a *Caucus on Biblically informed Missions* was held at Four Brooks Conference Center, Bucks County, Pennsylvania, between July 9 and 11, 1985. The following Statement was issued at the end of the assembly:

BECAUSE the uniqueness of the Christian Faith is being compromised by the movement called *Contextualization*, as advocated by many, which increasingly places cultural considerations above Biblical norms; and

BECAUSE the integrity of the Christian Gospel is being nullified by contextualized attempts to *build bridges* to non-Christian religions and to find common salvation-ground with them; and

BECAUSE the well being of the Christian Mission to earth's billions is being jeopardized by the development of *ethno-theologies* that would avoid the reproach of Christ and the offence of the Cross.

IT IS IMPERATIVE that an alarm be sounded and a standard raised for the rallying of those concerned with the fulfilling of the *Great Commission in a truly Biblical context.*

ACCORDINGLY,

1. WE AFFIRM the sovereignty of the Living Triune God in world evangelization and Gospel response, REJECTING any ultimate dependence on human means and methods of communication;

2. WE AFFIRM the sufficiency of the Biblical revelation, carried home by the Holy Spirit, to bring lost men and women to saving faith in Christ, REJECTING cultural accommodations which obscure, alter or relativize the Gospel, God's power unto salvation to everyone who believes;

3. WE AFFIRM the plain sense of holy scripture as normative for Christian discipleship and duty, REJECTING sophisticated reinterpretations by self-styled experts, which falsely stimulate missionary activity and deflect from true Gospel obedience;

4. WE AFFIRM that for historic Christianity, love for the lost and the unity of believers are always based on Scriptural truth, REJECTING concepts of love, which are contrary to truth and righteousness;

5. WE AFFIRM that faithfulness to God's revealed Word is the key to lasting God-honoring results in homelands and on mission fields, REJECTING concepts of love, which are contrary to truth and righteousness;

6. WE AFFIRM the primacy of Gospel proclamation over all other forms of Christian service, REJECTING theologies of mission, which would reduce evangelism to a parity with social action;

7. WE AFFIRM the believing church to be God's appointed means for the accomplishing of his purposes, REJECTING approaches that would bypass faithful, albeit imperfect, congregations in lands where the church has already been planted;

8. WE AFFIRM the importance of Christian workers identifying themselves as fully as possible with those to whom they would go with the Gospel, REJECTING, however any identification, which violates or obscures both the letter and spirit of scripture;

9. WE AFFIRM as those with a particular concern for the Islamic world, the long history of Christian missions to Muslims and rejoice in the many accomplishments, REJECTING the charge of general failure due to a lack of 'proper contextualization';

10. WE AFFIRM the responsibility of Christ's servants to declare to Muslims and all others the Christian message with precision and consistency; REJECTING appeals that would minimize, or seek to obliterate, the essential differences between Christianity and any other religion;

11. WE AFFIRM the unique Person, final authority and transcendent glory of Jesus Christ, our Great God and Savior, apart from Whom there is no salvation; REJECTING all comparisons between Him and the founders of other religious systems; and

12. WE AFFIRM the completeness of the redemptive work of Christ and the utter graciousness of his redemption, REJECTING any confusion of the Biblical revelation with so-called 'redemption analogies' in other religions/cultures of the world.

IN SUPPORT OF THESE AFFIRMATIONS, we would declare:

OUR COMMITMENT to further the Gospel of the grace of God by all means that are consistent with Biblical principles and Biblical ethics, this with a view to fulfilling Christ's supreme will for his church in this age; and

OUR COOPERATION with all who would advance God's work in God's way for God's glory, whom we invite to join hands and hearts with us that together we might reach out ever more effectively to the peoples of the earth with the Gospel of Christ; and

OUR CONFIDENCE that the victory of the gospel in the hearts and lives of a vast multitude out of all nations and kindred and people and tongues is assured by the Resurrection triumph of our Lord Jesus Christ, by the convicting and converting power of the Holy Spirit, and by the good will of God the Father.

IN TESTIMONY TO WHICH, and in the fervent hope that like-minded believers will stand with us in our affirmations, we herewith subscribe our names.

(copied with permission from http://levant.info/MER027.html)

Appendix 2

Insider Movements in West Java, Indonesia: A Case Study

Roger Dixon[1]

INTRODUCTION

WEST JAVA HAS PLAYED a critical role in the development of the *new insider* philosophy, which is different from the historical understanding of insider. The C1–C6 Spectrum, for example, originated from a worker in West Java.[2] Although this case study cannot give an in-depth analysis of how the *insider* philosophy developed in West Java, it does give an outline that will guide others in understanding the general development of the philosophy in that area.

The national team I work with advises workers to focus on the majority open people and not on the minority and most conservative religious block. In Indonesia, most Muslims are oriented to folk religions/spiritism and have a bent toward their indigenous cultures with some Islamic traits. There are only about thirty percent of these who are active in the mosque. About seventy percent of the Muslims (by the estimation of the Muslim leaders) are primarily nominal. So practically all the response in Indonesia has been among those who are only nominal Muslims. Islam

---

1. Roger Dixon, PhD, intercultural studies, Biola University; ThM, Fuller School of World Missions; MDiv, The Theological School, Drew University; BA, Randolph-Macon College; 34 years of residence in Muslim communities in S.E. Asia; 12 years of non-resident ministry; Church Planting coach; associate with Pioneers.

I am indebted to Roger for this case study that shows the tremendous problems that surround IM. [jm]

2. West Java is the home to about thirty-five million Muslim Sundanese. The Christian population is under one percent.

is not answering their spiritual questions so they will listen to the gospel. However, baptism is a major step few are willing to take.

There are some disclaimers to this case study. I was in West Java from 1985–1987 when the first workers who later inaugurated the insider philosophy in West Java arrived. I was also there from 1990–1998 when the insider philosophy blossomed. However, I was not there when certain critical events took place, which I will mention later. Therefore, let me state from the outset that this case study has weaknesses and merely forms a framework that others can use to investigate further. I have attempted to separate facts from my opinions. This is in no way a concise account of the entire story of the insider workers in West Java. There are many facts known only to those who promoted and propagated the teaching and implementation of the process. I appreciate the contributions of colleagues to this report.

Also, I have decided not to identify the workers by name even though none of those mentioned are still in West Java. I am doing this not to shield them but as a courtesy because many of them do not want their real names used in print and because they might have changed their views since then. I do mention John Travis (a pseudonym) because he has published.[3]

INSIDER MOVEMENT INITIATORS

While it was not known by any term at that time, some missionaries brought the basic teaching that has become known as the Insider Movements to West Java in the latter part of the 1980's. These missionaries came with Frontiers, Navigators, and Overseas Crusades (OC); but not all of the missionaries with these organizations were involved in insider practices. These new workers did not seem to me to have any apparent agenda at that time. It was only as time passed that their agenda became clear: they wanted to impose an Arabic model of Islamic outreach on an Asian/mystic worldview. At first most missionaries gave them the benefit of the doubt when it came to assessing their orthodoxy even though there were some who were suspicious.

---

3. You are welcome to email me if you need their names: rogerd205@gmail.com.

ARRIVAL OF THE NEW MISSIONARIES

Because of the new Indonesian government policies concerning missionaries, many of the pre-1980 generation left Indonesia. These were primarily missionaries with denominational boards and long time faith missions. The new wave of missionaries was not registered as such and they called themselves *tentmakers*. Their visas were secular and they had no responsibility or accountability to Indonesian churches or Christian agencies. This lack of church leadership that could mentor them became a serious flaw in their mode of approach. One of them recounted to me that he had not visited the Sundanese Bible school leader in his early years in the province. They were winging their way through ministry without experienced and reliable national advisors. Instead, they connected with young converts and others who would follow their directions.

In 1983, Frontiers put their first missionary in West Java and others followed shortly thereafter. This group grew quite large and some of their workers were the primary proponents of the new insider philosophy. The Navigators also brought new missionaries to the work. This agency had been in West Java since 1969 but had only one couple involved in Sundanese ministry. OC was another mission that had missionaries in West Java, but did not do church planting, though they trained and influenced various church planters. These were the three groups that began and/or gave significant support to what would be called insider approaches. After the movement started other agencies that were influenced and participated in lesser ways were the IMB, C&MA, YWAM, AG, and Australian Baptist.

CHARACTERISTICS OF THE MISSIONARIES

The new missionaries were energetic and had a variety of skills that they brought to the work. Typical of Americans, they were confident that they could start churches in a short period of time. One mentioned three years as the outside time he would expect to start a new church plant. Their desire for a quick change was characteristic of the boomer generation. They were not interested in applying the various models that had been implemented successfully by previous generations. A colleague adds the following:

> Also, like typical Americans, we (I will include myself in this generation of new arrivals) came in with an over-confidence in our

ability to do what previous generations had failed to do: foster a fast-growing movement amongst the Sundanese. The *new* tools in our toolbox included cutting edge concepts like *people movements, redemptive analogies,* and *contextualization* . . . that had us thinking about new approaches where our predecessors had got it wrong (this included the local church as well as traditional missionaries). The way that *contextualization* was conceptualized was often very truncated—being limited to Islamic forms, or the use of Arabic language/terms with the anticipation of receiving a greater amount of legitimacy within the host culture.

This presentation of *contextualization* often had the consideration of being the key to fruitfulness—or so it seemed even in the literature we imbibed before arriving on the field (for us, 1990). My limited observation would be that the lack of immediate results related to this level of contextualization resulted in my peers looking deeper into religious forms for the answer (i.e. becoming *more* Islamic was the key to greater fruitfulness) – thus initiating a slippery slope that led to one mission agency (Australian Baptists) effectively purging their ranks of members who were not willing to convert to Islam (note: I think that they have backed away from this experiment, but am not sure of their exact posture at this juncture).[4]

Another colleague adds that some workers came with the intention of establishing the C5 work because they viewed it as the purest form of Muslim church planting. This would certainly be true of most who came after 1990. Two missionaries in our area went to the mosque and recited the *shahada* to convert to Islam. Reports came from other areas of similar *conversions,* that were, sad to say, deceptions on the part of the missionaries.

The first of the missionaries from Frontiers did spend considerable time learning about what was being done in contextual church planting. He learned about the use of indigenous language, ceremonies, music, and other arts that were already being used in the Sundanese churches. But against the advice of the Sundanese evangelists, he also participated in the local martial arts known as *Silat.* This seemed to lead him to more openness in the use of Muslim musicians to produce Christian music recordings.

In July 1986, one of their members was denounced in the citywide ministers' meeting because he had drawn away a member of a local church

4. Email from a colleague, November 3, 2011.

when he evangelized him and recruited him to be a part of a church plant. This was an issue we had to address in order to prevent the tentmaker from being exposed to the government. Others from these new groups seemed to fear Muslim opposition to their message and they were willing to compromise with an Islamic-appropriate message. One member of Frontiers told me that after three years in the area, he had not evangelized anyone. Some seemed hesitant in talking about Jesus to Muslims.

By 1990, the Frontiers agency had six units in West Java but they found that it was difficult to start a church from Sundanese converts.

A lack of knowledge of Indonesian history was a basic problem for the new missionaries. It seemed that they did not want to take time to study the complicated history or culture of the many ethnic groups that formed the local Christian population. They did not carefully study the church model used in West Java. They were only interested in applying a model they thought would work but did not have the skills to do it. My colleague adds the following: "Indeed, there was a general bias against the local church, and a distancing from it, because of the poor reputation that Christians had (or were understood to have) in the general Muslim population. A Frontiers worker in Bogor said in a meeting of missionaries right before he returned to the US that he needed to repent for not working with the local church. He said that he was biased against it and it was a terrible mistake."[5]

NATURE OF THE PROVINCE

The development of Sundanese ministry has been slow and small throughout the history of the gospel in West Java. Most of the workers among the Sundanese were trying to follow the model of the Javanese church that had resulted in millions of Muslims coming to Christ. Historically, the largest turning of Muslims in the world has been among the Javanese. The Javanese confess when they become believers and they join the Christian church. In turn, they witness to their family, friends, and neighbors and others are brought to Christ through their witness. But our work among the Sundanese was slow even though they have a similar ethnic identity with the Javanese. However, by 1985, a vibrant ministry was planting churches successfully using the Javanese church-planting model with slight modifications.

5. Email to author from Matt Kirkus, January 1, 2012.

Appendix 2   113

INTRODUCTION OF THE BANGLADESH MODEL

Even before the Bangladesh model was introduced, some of the Frontiers' group were reworking the Bible to change the names and places so that they would correspond with Islamic designations. Abraham was changed to *Ibrahim*, etc. I do not know where this idea started. This did not concern us too much because the Indonesian language has always accommodated Arabic words and even the word *Isa* had been commonly used in various Christian publications such as songbooks. However, this was a foreshadowing of an aberrant New Testament translation.

Some time prior to 1990, as early as 1988 (I was not there at that time), someone introduced the Bangladesh model to the Frontiers missionaries. When I returned to West Java, it was being discussed in inter-agency meetings that included the IMB, OC, Navigators, and Pioneers. The Pioneers agency cooperated with an indigenous mission that employed the Javanese model and never got involved in insider strategy. It was the only agency of any size not to participate in some way. Interestingly, the Navigator agency was the only one with significant results using insider approaches. This was due to a dynamic missionary evangelist. He learned the Sundanese language fairly well and gathered many families of Muslims in nearby villages and discipled them with his agency's well known discipleship model. They also used employment to keep people in their model. Anyone who left their model lost their job in their furniture factory.

THE NEW INSIDER MODEL

In early 1991 a Frontiers missionary introduced the C1–C6 Spectrum as a model to evaluate the contextualization level of an indigenous church. The Frontiers' team wanted all of us to use the C5 category of this model in our ministries. One person told me that I should pull my *people* in line to use this model. My reply was that I did not have *people* that I controlled in outreach. The Indonesian evangelists would have to make their own decisions. The Indonesian evangelists with whom I worked strongly rejected the Islamic model.

Steve Richardson, President of Pioneers USA, comments: "In early discussions of the C scale, it was strongly presented as a descriptive rather than a prescriptive model. It wasn't long, however, before this seemed to change. Increasingly, some workers (expat and Indonesian) began referring to the *C5 approach* as a yardstick by which to gauge the effectiveness and validity of various ministries."[6]

Phil Parshall visited in August 1990 and in 1991. David Garrison came in January 1991 and J. Dudley Woodberry in March. Woodberry also came again in August of 1994 and it was only then that I realized his role in the insider movements. I consider the reporting of tens of thousands of Muslim converts in Bangladesh to be the basic motivation for the insider model in West Java. This report was accepted blindly by many inexperienced tentmakers even though many of us advised caution in believing stories of massive Muslim conversions. We had heard numerous reports like that before and the official results of the Bangladesh survey were never circulated to those best prepared to evaluate it. *The Bangladesh report has since been questioned and discredited, but the insider model upon which it is based continues.*[7]

The impact of the insider philosophy was strong after these visits convinced most of the agencies that Bangladesh was a legitimate model of church planting for West Java. There was another series of inter-agency meetings ostensibly to discuss ways to work together. In retrospect, it seems these meetings were actually organized to indoctrinate all the agencies in the insider philosophy brought over from the Bangladesh model. Woodberry's claims were touted as the proof that a great turning of Muslims could be initiated in West Java. Most of the new missionary groups wanted to implement this model in West Java, but they did not want to spend considerable time discussing the pros and cons of such a model for Indonesia.

In October 1993, I met a Chinese architect in Singapore who called himself Ibrahim. At times he wore robes like a Muslim cleric. He was even trying to grow a beard like some Muslims have. He had been to Bangladesh and was enthralled by the reports of massive conversion there. He wanted to replicate it in Singapore, but ultimately he was not able to do so. He shared about 60 pages of materials with me, asking that I not share them openly as they needed security. It included "Building Ishmaelite Growth Group Congregations," "Namaz Prayers," and "Fostering Messianic Kingdom Communities Among Dispersed Muslim Asians in Urban Centres." I filed it, as requested, but never used it because

---

6. Email to author, November 17, 2011.

7. This is Woodberry's case study to which I refer in chapter 10. [jm]

I considered it inappropriate. This was one of the experiences that made me realize that the insider philosophy was something more widespread than I had thought.

I can illustrate the seriousness of the new missionaries' commitment by relating a visit with a couple from the Frontiers' team. In tears, the wife told us that if we did not follow their model we would be causing millions of Sundanese to go to hell. At that time, I counseled her to be careful about being so emotional because none of us could carry the burden for the life and death of Sundanese and trying to do so could cause emotional collapse. We could only share the gospel. Two years later, her husband conveyed her apology for her comments, but she was still convinced the Islamic appropriate model was the only correct one. Those supporting this insider model rejected my input because they did not want to discuss their model with those who disagreed. This same individualistic pattern was followed with Indonesian converts, as they were isolated from other Indonesian Christians.

A colleague comments that this is one of the most significant points about the insider group: "This is a point that should be brought out more. Essentially they are not open to having an honest dialogue about the model. They want to instruct you in it but are not willing to consider their errors or alternative approaches."[8]

From the early 90's it seemed that two of the missionaries spent considerable time teaching this model in many places in Indonesia and in nearby countries as well, trying to convince workers everywhere that this Islamic appropriate model was God's will for all to use. Others returned to the U.S. to work in various positions with their agencies and further influence them in using these methods even though they had not been successful in planting churches. Some of these signed the letter castigating me for my article in EMQ, "Identity Theft."[9]

Their pattern of cobbling together Christian and Islamic theology such as *messianic Muslims, fulfilled Muslims*, and praying in the mosque was so aberrant that we thought it would soon die out. But these strategists located other immature workers like themselves and influenced evangelism and church planting practices in many places. Plutarch wrote: "Where the lion's skin will not reach, you must patch it out with the fox's"

---

8. Email from Matt Kirkus, January 1, 2012.
9. *EMQ* 43:4 (October 2007).

(*Lives*). This seems to be the philosophy of insider activists. Christian theology is cobbled together with Islamic faith and practices to form a new *spectrum* of beliefs different from both. The *Lion* is given a bizarre addition in order to attract the *itching ears*.

LACK OF FRUIT

The odd thing is that until today, the Navigators agency has been the only one temporarily successful with any notable response due to this model and that accomplishment is probably due more to the charismatic leadership of their missionary rather than to the use of an Islamic model. After he left West Java, his work was afflicted with significant losses and is no longer impressive. Indonesian leaders of that work are attending traditional Indonesian churches rather than culturally similar churches. However, that teaching and influence continue to multiply through training programs in the Riau islands and in other locations such as Malang in East Java. Until now, no other agency in West Java has seen notable results using this insider model. During the past twenty-five years, Frontiers has put teams in three cities, but none of them were successful in church planting other than the gathering of a few believers of mixed ethnic and religious backgrounds. In fact, one team they formed with members from several agencies was expelled from Indonesia because of their lack of wisdom. Nevertheless, many in these agencies using insider practices continue to expound it as the best answer to reaching Muslims with the gospel. Some launch personal attacks on anyone who disparages the use of this model.

LACK OF TRANSPARENCY

Toward the mid-90's when it became apparent to the agencies espousing insider philosophy that other agencies were not going to be convinced, the cloak of secrecy fell over much of their work.[10] They claimed that the lack of transparency was important so that their innovative new approach would not be jeopardized by the influence of what they called *traditional* Christians. They proposed that they were the only ones doing contextual ministry because their new model was the only contextual one. This was a result of a failure to recognize that millions of Javanese Muslims came to

---

10. After all, the whole insider model tends to be predicated on secrecy.

Christ because of a contextual approach that was not Islamically oriented. Converts were instructed not to associate with Christians who used the name Jesus and other traditional Christian terms. At one point they ordered all the Indonesians in their network not to attend a Sundanese ministry networking gathering where groups from different parts of the province shared reports of their work.

It became impossible either to validate or challenge their claims of success because they would not share information. In addition, they negotiated a bizarre agreement with most of the missionaries from other agencies to let them censor any articles that were written about the insider work in West Java. This closed the door on much evaluation and research that should have been revealed to the larger missionary and church community. On the other hand, the insider people wrote articles and promoted their philosophy in many directions without consultation.

In February 1994, I wrote an article for the Sundanese Christian magazine in which I explained why Christians use the name of *Yesus* rather than *Isa*. God used the New Testament in Greek to evangelize the world of that time and he chose the name of *Yesus* rather than the Hebrew word. Therefore, we use *Yesus* rather than the Arabic *Isa* because God inspired its use by those who wrote the New Testament. This article made it apparent to all those using insider philosophy that I was not to be trusted with any information about their activities and I was no longer invited to their missionary gatherings.

WEAKNESS OF THE C1–C6 SPECTRUM

In 1996, I wrote an article for an Indonesian journal outlining the weaknesses of the C1–C6 Spectrum as an indicator of contextualization in Indonesian evangelism and church planting. I pointed out the narrowness of the Spectrum in a number of categories. Considering that Indonesian Muslims generally follow two integrated worldviews, the Spectrum does not reflect any accurate evaluation of their religious positions. They have a formal religion and an informal. The informal animistic religious model has practitioners as well as the Islamic model; and it is the most influential in everyday life. The C1–C6 Spectrum does not deal with many of the serious issues of contextualization in new church plants. When I later encountered a worker from OC, I asked him how things were going. His reply was: "They were going okay until you published that article."

The essential mistake of the new mission agencies was their failure to understand that indigenous converts are the ones who are supposed to develop contextual models that agree with scripture. It is not the job of the missionary to tell them what to do to contextualize the gospel. Importing a model from another country is not the answer. In the successful model developed among the Javanese in the late 1800s, the missionaries simply taught the scriptures and probed their meaning with the Javanese. The indigenous people then applied Bible teaching to their culture and developed the strong Javanese churches of today. The process took many decades.

UNBIBLICAL LITERATURE AND PRACTICES

By 1993, unbiblical literature and practices were emerging from this insider philosophy, but most of us still thought that this was the result of immature workers. We tried to correct the errors in tracts that the westerners were writing and publishing without proper supervision. But there were other serious matters such as advising Christian workers to change their identity cards to indicate they were Muslims. Converts were being advised to not change their identity cards to indicate they were Christian. A number of young indigenous workers being salaried by these agencies did change their identity cards. One Indonesian worker I know in a non-insider ministry returned from a training program led by the insider missionaries and began telling his community that he was a Muslim. As a result he did little evangelism for the following two years. Thankfully, the Holy Spirit finally brought him back to his former dynamic self.

Even though some former insider missionaries have repudiated their unbiblical positions and teaching, the influence of such teaching has continued. Some Indonesian evangelists talk of *Isa Pesantrens* (Jesus Muslim training schools) in glowing terms, although there is no evidence of ongoing success in these models. This kind of thinking was unheard of before the insider philosophy poisoned many young Indonesian Christians.

I earlier mentioned the Navigators' furniture factory; some of the insider outreach was in community development and they have had a considerable range of application when it comes to theology. For example, some have had secret baptisms and others continue calling themselves Muslim even after they are baptized. There have been reactions from both Muslims and Christians as to the ethics of such deception. In the mid-nineties, articles in the provincial newspaper written by Muslims were warning Muslims of some of these tactics.

For example, the Navigator organization set up a variation of the five prayer times a day in which the prayers were altered to be *Christianized*. They continued this practice even though advised against it by mature national Christian leaders. In addition, one of their own converts told them that it was a *return to bondage*. Unfortunately, listening to the converts' efforts to contextualize was not a strong point of most of these missionaries. They wanted the converts to follow the Bangladesh model they had imported as a *contextual* model.

After one baptism ceremony led by the Navigators group, I asked the missionary if he had taught them that Jesus was the Son of God. He replied that they would teach them that later in a series of Bible studies that they had prepared for new believers. I was stunned that they were baptizing people without any biblical basis. It was like the baptism of John mentioned in Acts 19:3–4. Without understanding the basis of forgiveness as being the work of the Son of God, they had no theological grounds for baptism.

THE EVOLUTION OF THE C1–C6 SPECTRUM

In the early presentations to the missionary community, the C1–C6 Spectrum was considered a descriptive model of what was happening in the Muslim world church planting. John Travis (a pseudonym for a Frontiers' missionary) had talked with mission leaders concerning events in other places and had also traveled and received reports from various workers in miscellaneous places. At its first appearance in 1991, the C in the C1–C6 Spectrum stood for church. It was supposed to be a picture of what kinds of churches were being formed in the Muslim world. When it was published in 1998,[11] it had morphed into a "practical tool for defining six types of 'Christ-centered communities.'" The C no longer stood for church. In this version, the word contextualize only appears under the description of C3 and C4 communities. But the impression is that the other communities are also *contextualized* models.

Long before the publication of his article, I tried to impress on Travis that the C1–C6 Spectrum was not a good model of contextualization or of any significance in describing church planting. It is flawed since

---

11. See *EMQ* 34(4): 407–8.

it describes "Christ-centered communities" as a mixture of Islam and Christianity (or Islamic and biblical features), thus alienating these communities from an accurate biblical community description. The C1–C6 Spectrum may have some diagnostic use, but it describes neither a church community nor a Christ-centered one.

However, for some the C1–C6 Spectrum is considered a prescriptive model rather than a description of what actually exists. Travis promoted C5 groups extensively. He gives this example: "As we have continued to see the limits of C4 in our context, and as our burden for lost Muslims only grows heavier, we have become convinced that a C5 expression of faith could actually be viable for our precious Muslim neighbors and probably large blocks of the Muslim world. We ourselves, being CBBs, maintain a C4 lifestyle, but we believe God has called us to help 'birth a C5 movement' in our context (this will be discussed later in this chapter).[12]

The model is clearly *prescriptive* rather than *descriptive*. The creator of C1–C6 thinking urges others to "birth a C5 movement" which, by implication, does not yet exist.

A FALSE NEW TESTAMENT

Probably the most serious damage caused by the insider group was done after I had moved from West Java. It was the publication of the New Testament in a form altered to be compatible with Islamic theology. The problem with this Bible is that it will be the only Bible available and thus converts will never be able to know what the true Word is. This was a project of the Frontiers agency and OC. It was first printed in 2000 as a diglot with the title *Kitab Suci Injil* (New Testament) and has been revised and reprinted in 2007 as a third edition with the same name and form. Its major oddity is retaining the inclusion of the Greek as a diglot even though the Greek is translated incorrectly in many cases. This is particularly true in the way it changes filial language and in reducing the impact of the designation of Jesus as Lord. He thus becomes a figure no higher than any honored teacher or leader.

Similar to the previous edition, the translators still use the secular word, *junjungan* for the Greek word for Lord, *kurios*. This word for Lord in Greek appears about 691 times in the New Testament. It also was used

---

12. Charles H. Kraft (Ed). *Appropriate Christianity*. Pasadena, California: William Carey Library, 2005. 401–2. CBB is a Christian Background Believer.

in the Greek Old Testament translation (*Septuagint*) to represent the Hebrew name of God, JHVH. In his article in *A Theological Wordbook of the Bible*, J.Y. Campbell points out "Paul boldly applies to Christ OT passages in which 'the Lord' meant God."[13] Arndt and Gingrich translate W. Bauer as having the same opinion: "*kurios* is also used in reference to Jesus . . . in OT quotations, where it is understood of the new Lord of the Christian church. . . . the use of the word k. raises Jesus above the human level."[14]

The translators of the *Kitab Suci Injil* add the Indonesian word for divine (*ilahi*) to this secular word *junjungan* when they want to emphasize the nature of Jesus. But there is no comparative use of such phrases in the Indonesian language because *junjungan* is a purely secular honorific word whether used for the prophet Mohammad or for the president of Indonesia. Historically, Bible translators in Indonesia used the word *Tuhan* to translate Lord because that Indonesian word has both divine and secular connotations. Nonetheless, the editors claim that this edition "still follows the original Greek text." The editors claim to follow the 1912 edition that was William Shellabear's translation. But fortunately, since Shellabear was actually strongly opposed to using Arabic and Islamic terms in his translation, they do not mention his name.

In a meeting with three missionaries in March 2006, John Travis admitted to my wife and me that they deliberately changed the wording in the Gospel of John so that Muslims would want to read it. And all of the missionaries present agreed that change was contrary to the intent of John's gospel. This confirmed for us that there was a conspiracy of sorts to shift (for however long) the identity of Jesus from his role as the second person of the trinity to one of an outstanding prophet. Some missionaries had caved to Muslim replacement theology where the identity of Jesus is changed to be simply one of Islam's prophets. However, an OC worker, who also promoted the translation, told me later that Travis was mistaken in what he said.

In 2007, I wrote "Identity Theft" in which I pointed out the errors in the 2000 edition of *Kitab Suci Injil*. This article created an extreme reaction from several groups and led to a letter published in *EMQ*, October,

---

13. J. Y. Campbell. "Kurios." In *A Theological Wordbook of the Bible* 1950:131.

14. Walter Bauer (1960). *A Greek-English Lexicon of the New Testament and other early Christian Literature*. William F. Arndt and F. Wilbur Gingrich, trans. Chicago: The University of Chicago Press.

2007, p.413, condemning me of slander. Members of the IMB, Frontiers, OC, C&MA, consultants from Wycliffe Bible Translators, and others all signed the document. This is not surprising since some of them were promoting and financing this publication. They justified using the terms *master* and *divine master* to translate Lord, but failed to address the issue of how the meaning of *Son of God* is eviscerated. I continue to condemn such publications where the person and work of Jesus is compromised in any way though I deny slandering the misguided translators. Stating one's opinion that another person's viewpoint is erroneous is not slander. I never said their motives were bad, only their scholarship.

In his commentary on 1 Corinthians, Thiselton references Tertullian concerning how Marcion changed the text in 1 Cor. 15:47: "Marcion changed *the second man* to Lord (*kurios*) for reasons of theology. Tertullian explicitly attacks Marcion's changing of the text for his own purposes: 'If *the first* was a *man*, can there be a second unless he were a *man* also? Or if *the second* is '*Lord*' was *the first* also '*Lord*'?' Here is an early witness to textual issues."[15]

The theological message from the early church fathers is clearly "do not change the text." Let God's word say what God says.

SITUATION TODAY: 2011

Most of the westerners who were the early promoters of the insider theology in West Java have left Indonesia though their unfortunate influence remains in some circles. Even missionaries from other Asian countries have been influenced to continue this model in parts of Indonesia. Many of the Indonesians as well as some of the missionaries who were attracted by the insider teaching have recognized its heretical aspects. As the Indonesians interact with Christians of sound biblical faith, they will be seeking to ground their faith in a biblical theology of the person and work of Jesus.

A few missionaries have made a sad witness to the gospel by following the Islamic model and saying the shahada and joining the mosque. One YWAM worker with whom I am acquainted has joined the mosque and now displays a significant change from his former joyful and engaging personality. As a friend of mine, who was formerly Muslim commented,

---

15. Anthony C. Thiselton. *The First Epistle to the Corinthians* NIGTC. Grand Rapids, Michigan: Eerdmans, 2000. 1285.

"The spirit of the mosque is a strong spirit." It is sad that some do not realize this, but instead promote behaviors that actually submit to that spirit.

On the whole, local churches in West Java do not seem to be affected by insider philosophy although there are a few large denominations that are involved. Very few of the pastors and leaders even know what it is. The new translations are not widely sold in Christian bookstores and they are not used in churches outside the insider circles. In fact, most Christian leaders are not even aware of the new translations. Because of their secrecy model, insider influence is probably felt in less than one percent of the churches—very much as it is in America.

However, there is still considerable danger in outreach to the unsaved. The churches interested in reaching the unevangelized ethnic groups in Indonesia will most likely be introduced to this philosophy at some time because the insider promoters seek out churches that are called to evangelize the unreached. This means that those who are being introduced to the gospel message are likely to be affected by insider theology because they are not able to distinguish which theology is biblical. The insider translation of the New Testament makes this even more difficult for the inquirer or new believer to understand which presentation of the gospel is biblical. This teaching needs to be eradicated and replaced with one that is biblical.

Bibliography

`Ali, `Abdullah, Yusuf, *The Meaning of the Holy Qur'an*. Beltsville, Maryland: Amana Publications, 1989.
Barnes, Albert. *Notes on the New Testament: 1 Corinthians*. No pages. Online. http://www.studylight.org/com/bnn/view.cgi?book=1co&chapter=007.
Belz, Emily. "Inside Out." *World*, May 7, 2011. No pages. http://www.worldmag.com/articles/17944.
Brogden, Dick. "Inside Out: Probing Presuppositions among Insider Movements." *IJFM* 27:1 (2010) 33–40.
Bruce, F. F. *The Book of Acts* NICNT. Grand Rapids, Michigan: Eerdmans, 1988.
Caldwell, Stuart. "Jesus in Samaria: A Paradigm for Church Planting Among Muslims." *IJFM* 17:1 (2000) 25–31.
Calvin, Jean. *Commentary on 1 Corinthians*. No pages. Online. http://www.ccel.org/ccel/calvin/ calcom39.xvi.i.html.
Chapman, Roger. "Cognitive Categories and Our Mission Approach." *Journal of Applied Missiology* 6:2 (October 1995) No pages. Online. http://www.bible.acu.edu/ministry/centers_institutes/missions/page.asp?ID=461.
Corwin, Gary. "A Humble Appeal to C5/Insider Movement Muslim Ministry Advocates to Consider Ten Questions." *IJFM* 24:1 (2007) 5–21.
Culver, Richard D. "Melchizedek." In *Theological Wordbook of the Old Testament*, vol. 1. Chicago: Moody Press, 1980.
Fernando, Ajith. *Acts* TNAC. Grand Rapids, Michigan: Zondervan, 1998.
Geisler, Norman L. and William E. Nix. *A General Introduction to the Bible* 2nd ed. Chicago, Illinois: Moody Press, 1986.
Hanson, Colin, "The Son and the Crescent." *Christianity Today* 55:2 (February 2011). No pages. http://www.christianitytoday.com/ct/2011/february/soncrescent.html.
Higgins, Kevin. "The Key to Insider Movements: The 'Devoted's' of Acts." *IJFM* 21:4 (2004) 155–65.
———. "Identity, Integrity and Insider Movements: A Brief Paper Inspired by Timothy C. Tennent's Critique of C-5 Thinking." *IJFM* 23:3 (2006) 117–23.
———. "Acts 15 and Insider Movements Among Muslims: Questions, Process, and Conclusions." *IJFM* 24:1 (2007) 29–40.
———. "Inside What? Church, Culture, Religion and Insider Movements in Biblical Perspective." *SFM* 5:4 (2009) 74–91.

Horrell, David G. "No Longer Jew or Greek: Paul's Corporate Christology and the Construction of Christian Community." University of Exeter ERIC website. Online. https://eric.exeter.ac.uk/repository/bitstream/handle/10036/3087/No%20longer%20Jew%20Greek.pdf?sequence=1.

Lewis, Rebecca. "Promoting Movements to Christ Within Natural Communities." *IJFM* 24:2 (2007) 75–76.

———. "Insider Movements: Honoring God-Given Identity and Community." *IJFM* 26:1 (2009) 16–19.

———. "The Integrity of the Gospel and Insider Movements." *IJFM* 27:1 (2010) 41–48.

Lingel, Joshua, Jeff Morton, and Bill Nikides. *Chrislam: How Missionaries are Promoting an Islamized Gospel*. Garden Grove, California: i2 Ministries, 2011.

Mallouhi, Mazhar. "Comments on the Insider Movement." *SFM* 5:5 (2009) 3–14.

Marshall, I. Howard. *The Acts of the Apostles* TNTC. Grand Rapids, Michigan: Eerdmans, 1980.

McDermott, Gerald R. *Can Evangelicals Learn from World Religions?* Downer's Grove, Illinois: InterVarsity Press, 2000.

Medearis, Carl. *Muslims, Christians and Jesus: gaining understanding and building relationships*. Minneapolis, Minnesota: Bethany House, 2008.

———. *Speaking of Jesus: the art of not-evangelism*. Colorado Springs, Colorado: David C. Cook, 2001.

PCA, Overture 9, 2011. "Toward a Faithful Witness." No pages. Online: http://www.pcaac.org/2011GeneralAssembly/Overture%209%20Potomac%20Faithful%20Witness%203-31-11.pdf.

Richard, H. L. "Unpacking the Insider Paradigm: An Open Discussion on Points of Diversity." *IJFM* 26:4 (2009) 175–80.

Robertson, A. T. *Word Pictures in the New Testament* 6 volumes. Nashville, Tennessee: Broadman Press, 1931.

Tannehill, Robert C. *The Narrative Unity of Luke–Acts: A Literary Interpretation* 2 volumes. Minneapolis, Minnesota: Fortress Press. 1990.

Tennent, Timothy. "Followers of Jesus (Isa) in Islamic Mosques: A Closer Examination of C-5 High Spectrum Contextualization." *IJFM* 23:3 (2006) 101–15.

Weerstra, Hans M. "Mission to the Nations: A Biblical Word Study of Ethnos." *IJFM* 9:3 (1992) 99–101.

www.ingramcontent.com/pod-product-compliance
Lightning Source LLC
Chambersburg PA
CBHW071858160426
43197CB00013B/2523